WHO'S
BETTER,
WHO'S
BEST IN
HOCKEY?

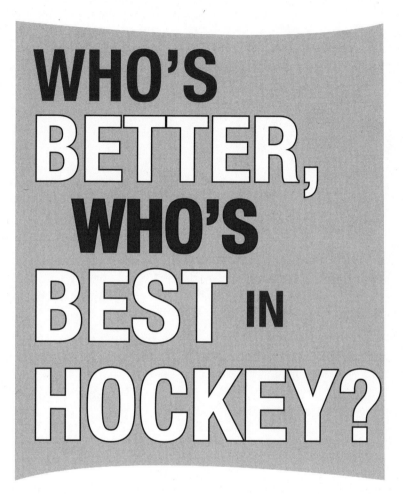

WHO'S BETTER, WHO'S BEST IN HOCKEY?

STEVE SILVERMAN

SPORTS
PUBLISHING

Sports Publishing books may be purchased in bulk at special discounts for sales promotion, corporate gifts, fund-raising, or educational purposes. Special editions can also be created to specifications. For details, contact the Special Sales Department, Sports Publishing, 307 West 36th Street, 11th Floor, New York, NY 10018 or sportspubbooks@skyhorsepublishing.com.

Sports Publishing® is a registered trademark of Skyhorse Publishing, Inc.®, a Delaware corporation.

Visit our website at www.sportspubbooks.com.

10 9 8 7 6 5 4 3 2

Library of Congress Cataloging-in-Publication Data is available on file.

Cover design by Tom Lau
Cover photo credit AP Images

ISBN: 978-1-61321-819-8
Ebook ISBN: 978-1-61321-847-1
Printed in the United States of America

To my children, Samantha and Gregory, and my beautiful grand-daughter, Anna.

CONTENTS

A NOTE ON POINT SHARES

You will notice throughout this book an advanced statistic called Point Shares.

Hockey, like the other three major sports, is going through a statistical revolution that provides coaches, scouts and analysts–as well as journalists, authors, and fans–a better way to evaluate a player's contribution.

There is no one stat–or advanced stat–that allows any individual to make a definitive call on any player's talent, ability, or contribution to the game.

However, advanced stats are helpful, and in the case of this sport, Point Shares is a solid measuring tool. It gives an objective look at a player's offensive and defensive contribution, as well as his overall contribution. It is used extensively by the Hockey-Reference website.

The Point Share statistic provides an avenue to measure a player's contribution and compare it to players from differing eras. During the 1988-89 season, Mario Lemieux led all scorers with an eye-opening 199 points. However, he had plenty of company at the top of the scoring list. Three other players—Wayne Gretzky, Steve Yzerman, and Bernie Nicholls—scored 150 or more points.

Compare that to the 2014-15 season, when Jamie Benn of the Dallas Stars won the scoring title with 87 points, edging out John Tavares, who notched 86 points.

Point Shares allows the comparison of players from those two seasons with their divergent scoring totals.

While the Point Shares ranking is not perfect—it doesn't allow consideration for Bobby Orr's injury-shortened career—it is an important stat that was quite helpful in preparing the rankings in this book.

#1

Bobby Orr

Ten seasons with Boston Bruins. Two seasons with Chicago Blackhawks.

He is simply the greatest player ever. From the moment Bobby Orr stepped on the ice for the Boston Bruins, there was something different about the way he played and the way he skated.

The only thing that didn't come with this tremendous gift was good health. Instead of skating in the NHL for twenty-plus years like superstar defenseman Ray Bourque, who would follow him in Boston, Orr lasted just twelve seasons.

Career regular season:
657 games, 270 goals, 645 assists, 915 points
Three-time Hart Trophy winner (MVP)
Two-time Ross Trophy winner (Leading Scorer)
Two-time Conn Smythe Trophy winner (Playoff MVP)
Eight-time Norris Trophy winner (Best Defenseman)
One-time Calder Trophy winner (Rookie of the Year)
One-time Ted Lindsay Award winner (Most Outstanding Player)
Eight-time first-team NHL All-Star; one-time second-team NHL All-Star
Two-time Stanley Cup winner
Elected to Hall of Fame in 1979
Advanced stats: 90.1 OPS, 61.9 DPS, 152.0 PS

Tornados, hurricanes, snowstorms, and blizzards don't need a lot of time to inflict their damage, and neither did Orr.

The Bruins brought Orr to Boston in 1966–67 and his last relatively healthy season in Boston was 1974–75. He was able to play a short time in 1975–76 for the Bruins, and then moved on to the Chicago Blackhawks for short runs in 1976–77 and 1978–79. Those trials revealed that Orr could no longer skate at any level close to what he had done in the past and led to his tearful goodbye to the sport.

But while he was healthy—or at least relatively so—there was a phenomenal ability to control play and create with his skating, stick-handling, playmaking, shooting, and defending.

Orr was a defenseman who reinvented the position. Prior to his arrival with the Bruins, defensemen were expected to retrieve the puck, get it out of the defensive zone, pass it to forwards, and hang back at the blue line.

Orr would have none of those limitations on his game. From the earliest age—when he was a tow-headed youngster skating against older stars—he would get the puck on his stick and go. He would skate up ice, carry it past the red line, find an open teammate, and deliver a perfect pass and take one in return to create a scoring opportunity. Perhaps he would weave through two or three defenders, hold on to the puck the entire time, and simply shoot and score.

He did what he wanted to do within the team concept. Orr had gifts that might have made others jealous, but he never had any of the diva tendencies that so many of the superstars outside of the sport of hockey have. His talent had nothing to do with the way he interacted with his teammates or the public. He was enveloped by an air of decency that made him even more of a hero to the people of Boston.

Orr came along before the NHL held its first common draft, and the Bruins had discovered him while on a scouting trip to look at another player in Parry Sound, Ontario. However, when scout Wren Blair got a glimpse of Orr skating with the puck, he knew he had seen a player who could turn around the fortunes of the Bruins by his mere presence.

Orr quickly put his talents on display with the junior A team in Oshawa as a fourteen-year-old. He was just 5-6 and 135 pounds and playing against grown men, and he made the second-All-Star team even though he didn't attend a single practice.

He kept growing and became more dominant, and by the time his junior career was over, Orr was 6-0 and a 200-pound man. Bruins fans were bursting with hope at a chance to see Orr play and find out if he was really as good as his legend.

His first game as a Bruin was quite the introduction. Orr and the Bruins played Gordie Howe and the Detroit Red Wings. After getting introduced to the game by one of Howe's patented elbows, Orr registered an assist, blocked shots, moved Red Wings players away from the net, and delivered hard checks. He dominated the defensive part of the game and he skated like the wind.

By the end of his rookie season, Orr had scored 13 goals and 28 assists, won the Calder Trophy, made the NHL's second All-Star team, and finished third in Norris Trophy voting and sixth in the Hart Trophy race. New York Rangers defenseman Harry Howell won the Norris Trophy that season, and had this prescient remark.

"I'm glad I won the award now, because it's going to belong to Bobby Orr from now on," Howell said.

Howell knew exactly what he was talking about, as Orr would win the award as the league's best defenseman for eight straight seasons.

Bobby Hull was equally impressed by Orr after seeing him the first time. Orr's speed and ability to control play had led the Blackhawks' superstar to remark that two pucks were needed in any game against the Bruins. "Orr can have one and the rest of us can have the other one," Hull said.

The Bruins had been in a deep funk through the beginning of the 1960s, as they had missed the playoffs from 1959–60 through Orr's arrival. However, prior to the 1967–68 season, they made a trade with the Chicago Blackhawks that brought them Phil Esposito, and that acquisition gave them the goal scorer they needed to take advantage of Orr's speed and dexterity.

After the Bruins went 17-43-10 in Orr's rookie season, they went 37-27-10 in his second year and became a playoff fixture. While they could not get by the Montreal Canadiens in the first round of the playoffs, it was clear that the Bruins were the NHL's team on the rise.

Orr was limited to 46 games in his second season as a result of injuries, but he still scored 11 goals and 20 assists. However, he turned into Orr, the legend, the following season.

Orr's third season in the NHL is when he truly asserted himself. He scored 21 goals and 43 assists in winning his second straight Norris Trophy. He was in the lineup for 67 games, and his 65 points meant he nearly scored a point a game, which was simply unheard of for a defenseman.

When the regular season concluded, the Bruins were in second place with 100 points, just three points behind Montreal. The Bruins trounced Toronto in four straight games in the first round, winning the first two games in Boston by a 10-0 and 7-0 margin.

However, the Canadiens stopped them in six games in the next round, and their inability to contend with the Habs in those first two playoff years was part of a trend that had started in the 1940s and would continue until 1988, well after Orr's retirement.

Bobby Orr

The 1969–70 season saw the Big, Bad Bruins come to full maturity. They were a marauding bunch that beat opponents and regularly used their physical dominance to intimidate them.

The Bruins and Blackhawks tied for the league lead in points with 99, but Chicago had more victories and that was the tie-breaking factor when it came to determining the East Division championship and home-ice advantage.

The Bruins cared little. Orr had gone from remarkable player the previous year to supernova in 1969–70 by scoring 33 goals and 87 assists as he won the Hart Trophy as well as the Norris Trophy.

The Bruins had developed a rivalry with the New York Rangers, a team that had also shown significant improvement. The two teams were often viewed as near-equals, but the Bruins had Orr, swagger, and a real edge to their game that the Rangers lacked.

Boston beat New York in a tough six-game series in the opening round. From there, it was a cakewalk to the team's first Stanley Cup since 1939. They whipped the Chicago Blackhawks in four straight games and did the same with the Western Conference champion St. Louis Blues in the Stanley Cup Final.

The Bruins beat the Blues easily in the first three games of the series, but St. Louis had come up with an extra effort in Game 4 at the steamy Boston Garden on Mother's Day in 1970. The score was tied at 3-3 after 60 minutes, and the Bruins would need overtime to secure the victory.

It came on the most memorable play of Orr's career. Early in overtime, Orr gathered a puck along the boards in the St. Louis zone and took two strides with it before sending it behind the net to teammate Derek Sanderson. The colorful center hit Orr with a pass on the tape of his stick blade and goalie Glenn Hall's legs opened up as Orr received the puck. He shoveled the puck between the goalie's legs and the Bruins had their victory.

As they celebrated and roared, history had been made. Not so much by Orr, but by *Boston Herald* photographer Ray Lussier, who captured the most famous image in hockey history. At the instant Orr made his series-clinching shot, St. Louis defenseman Noel

Picard went between Orr's skates and tripped him. However, instead of falling to the ice, the trip propelled the leaping Orr into the air. He flew like Superman, and Orr's famous "Flying Goal" was preserved on film forever.

The Bruins had the look of a dynasty the following year as they rolled to a 57-14-7 record for 121 points that earned a 12-point edge over the second-place Rangers. The Bruins scored 399 goals that year in 78 regular season games, and that was 108 goals more than Montreal, the second-highest scoring team in the league.

By all rights, the Bruins should have rolled to a second straight Stanley Cup because of their high-scoring ways. However, they were beaten in seven games by the Habs once again, and the Bruins were left in stunned silence.

Orr had been brilliant with 37 goals and 102 assists to win his second straight Hart Trophy, and he was devastated by the loss. He came back the following season to tally 37 goals and 80 assists. While not quite as high-scoring—just 330 goals that year—the team returned more disciplined and determined than the previous season.

They beat the Maple Leafs in five games in the opening round, swept the Blues in the second round, and won the championship by beating an excellent Rangers team in six games.

Orr was the difference in the Final, and he picked up his second Conn Smythe Trophy. Orr had helped convert the rollicking Bruins into a finely tuned machine, and while they were never a dynasty, the two championship teams in the three-year period from 1970 through 1972 were as exciting as the NHL has ever seen.

Orr would have three more brilliant years before his ravaged knees prevented him from being the game-changing defenseman any longer. His 1974–75 season was particularly brilliant from an offensive point of view, as he scored 46 goals and 89 assists for a league-high 135 points.

The end was sad and not particularly swift.

He played just 10 games for the Bruins in 1975–76, and he signed a free-agent deal with the Blackhawks prior to the 1976–77 season.

Bobby Orr

He played 20 games that year and six games two years later before he tearfully called it quits.

However, there would be one more brilliant display in 1976 as Orr suited up for Canada in the international Canada Cup competition. He scored two goals and seven assists in seven games even though he was not the same athlete he had been.

"He's the best guy out here," said longtime rival Bobby Clarke. "And he's skating on one leg."

That was Orr in a nutshell. He had been the most gifted athlete the game had ever known, and he coupled his gifts with a hunger and a desire to always be at his best no matter what kind of impediments were placed in his way.

There will never be another like him.

#2

Wayne Gretzky

NHL: Ten seasons with Edmonton Oilers (1 WHA, 9 NHL). Eight seasons with Los Angeles Kings. Three seasons with New York Rangers. One season with St. Louis Blues. One Season with Indianapolis Racers (WHA) .

Wayne Gretzky has won every contest he's ever been in when it comes to superiority on the ice. To many, there is no question that he was the greatest player ever, and his records seemingly go on for miles.

However, while we don't want to get into a spitting contest with those who question our choice of Bobby Orr as the best ever over Gretzky, we offer this point. When *The Hockey News* named its fifty greatest players ever in 1997, it gave Gretzky the nod and former Oiler coach and general manager Glen Sather offered this illuminating point. "There aren't enough adjectives. Just look at his records and longevity."

Ahh, longevity. Gretzky had it, and Orr didn't. We are not going to punish Orr because injured knees denied him a lengthy career and a miraculous prime. Gretzky had good health throughout his career, and he took advantage of it to the hilt. He is the most brilliant of offensive talents and it's difficult to split the two in greatness and importance.

However, for the purpose of this book, it had to be done and the nod went to Orr.

Career regular season:
NHL: 1,487 games, 894 goals, 1,963 assists, 2,857 points
WHA: 80 games, 46 goals, 64 assists, 110 points
10-time Art Ross Trophy winner (Leading Scorer)
Nine-time Hart Trophy winner (MVP)
Five-time Ted Lindsay Award winner (Most Outstanding Player)
Five-time Lady Byng Trophy (Gentlemanly Play)
Two-time Conn Smythe Trophy winner (Playoff MVP)
One-time Lou Kaplan Trophy winner (WHA rookie of the year)
Eight-time first-team NHL All-Star; seven-time second-team NHL All-Star
One-time second-team WHA All-Star
Four-time Stanley Cup winner
Elected to Hall of Fame in 1999
Advanced stats: 223.9 OPS, 27.1 DPS, 251.0 PS

★ ★ ★

Gretzky's amazing career began as a child prodigy. Growing up in Brantford, Ontario, young Wayne loved to be on skates at his local park. He spent so much time there that his father built him a backyard hockey rink of his own.

Walter Gretzky had grown tired of taking his young son to the park and enduring the cold. By building one on his property, Walter could watch his son from the comfort of his home.

The youngster was machine-like when it came to practicing his beloved sport. From skating, to stickhandling, passing, and shooting, he simply dominated, and before long six- and seven-year-old Gretzky was outplaying older players and climbing the ladder to excellence.

No matter what youth league he played in, Gretzky regularly showed that his play was superior, even if players were bigger, stronger, and older.

Gretzky became a national phenomenon when he scored 378 goals in his last season of pee wee hockey in his hometown. From that point on, Gretzky was a celebrity who was destined for hockey greatness.

He dominated international competitions while playing for Canada, and he was the leading scorer in the World Junior Championships played in Quebec as a sixteen-year-old. This competition has often been the birthplace to NHL stars of the future; in Gretzky's case, it was just confirmation that superstardom was inevitable.

Gretzky wanted the opportunity to go pro as early as possible, and that meant signing a contract with the World Hockey Association's Indianapolis Racers prior to the 1978–79 season at the age of seventeen. However, that team was just about to go under, and owner Nelson Skalbania sold Gretzky to the Edmonton Oilers after just eight games in Indianapolis.

Gretzky flourished in Edmonton, as he got the chance to play with superior talent in Mark Messier, Jari Kurri, Paul Coffey, Glenn Anderson, and Grant Fuhr. It was clear that the young Oilers were about to become a great team, and while all of his teammates were on their way to becoming legitimate superstars, it was Gretzky who shined the brightest.

As an eighteen-year-old with the Oilers, he scored 43 goals and 61 assists in 72 games in the last season of the WHA. He won that league's rookie of the year honors, and the Oilers got to the WHA's

Wayne Gretzky

Avco Cup Final—that league's equivalent of the Stanley Cup—before losing to the Winnipeg Jets.

The following year, the Oilers were admitted to the NHL, and they became a playoff team in their first year. Much of that was due to Gretzky, who was simply unstoppable when he had the puck.

Gretzky did not present like a phenomenon or a game changer, but that's just what he was. Gretzky looked almost frail when he stepped onto the ice compared to the other players, but as soon as he took his first steps, it was clear that he was in control of all the action.

Gretzky had remarkable skating quickness and balance. While his end-to-end speed was not his best attribute, Gretzky was able to reach top speed quickly and dart away from defenders. He also had an incredible knack for getting to loose pucks, controlling them, and then making a play that nobody else could conceive of, let alone execute.

That ability came from all the hours that he had spent practicing the game as a youngster. He dominated the NHL offensively as no player before or since has ever done. He scored 51 goals and 85 assists in 1979–80, the Oilers' first year in the NHL. That performance earned him the Hart Trophy as well as the Lady Byng Award.

But as impressive as that performance was, it paled in comparison to what he would do over the next seven years. Gretzky would turn the NHL into his own personal playground with remarkable and explosive scoring. He would break the 50-goal mark in 1980-81 and again the following year, and he piled up 137 and 164 points, respectively, in those two seasons.

The next year, he would accomplish the remarkable feat of scoring 92 goals in a season. The previous record had been 76 goals by Boston's Phil Esposito in 1970–71, and many thought it would last for decades. Gretzky obliterated it. He also scored his 50th goal that year in his 39th game. None of the greats who had preceded Gretzky could even conceive of that kind of scoring, at that kind of pace. For all of Gretzky's ability as a goal scorer—he did it with timing, quick hands, a brilliant release, and accuracy, but not sheer velocity—it was his passing that was probably his best quality. He added 120 assists for a mind-boggling 212 points in 1981–82.

Gretzky exceeded the 200-point mark in three of the next four seasons, and he went to new heights in the assist category in 1985–86. Gretzky accumulated 163 assists that year—along with 52 goals—and set the single-season scoring record with 215 points.

While Gretzky and the Oilers were lighting up scoreboards around the NHL nearly every night, they were getting somewhat frustrated in the playoffs. While they were getting better every year, they had not been able to claim the Stanley Cup through the 1982–83 season. The New York Islanders were in the midst of a dynastic run, and they stopped the Oilers in four games in the Final.

It was a painful defeat for Gretzky and the Oilers, but it was not one they would have to live with for a long time. They were back in the championship round the following year against the four-time champion Islanders, but this time there would be no denying them.

The Oilers got their revenge in 1984, winning the series in five games. After that, nobody could beat the Oilers—except the Oilers.

After winning the Stanley Cup again in 1985 over the Philadelphia Flyers, they were expected to roll through the playoffs in 1986. However, after a first-round victory over the Vancouver Canucks, the Oilers lost to the Calgary Flames in seven games on a fluke goal late in the final game. Defenseman Steve Smith had the puck behind the Edmonton net, and as he started to skate with it, he accidentally sent the puck off of Fuhr's skate and into the net for the decisive goal in the series.

The Oilers came back to win the title in 1987 and '88. The '88 championship run was Gretzky's last with the Oilers.

Owner Peter Pocklington was having some financial problems, and that led him to consider moving Gretzky. The Los Angeles Kings were more than happy to move heaven and earth to acquire Gretzky and that's just what they did.

Losing Gretzky did not derail the Oilers though, as they won yet another title in 1990, but the loss of Gretzky was seen as something of a national tragedy in Canada. While Gretzky, his Edmonton teammates, and much of the nation's fans were heartbroken, he came to Los Angeles and basically established a sport that had often seemed foreign to the Southern California culture.

Gretzky had brilliant years with the Kings and even led them to the 1993 Stanley Cup Final, but they could not overcome the Montreal Canadiens. He finished his brilliant career with a three-year run with the New York Rangers that ended in the 1998–99 season.

Slower in those final seasons, Gretzky was still a brilliant passer and a game-changer until the end. He left his last game to a tearful ovation from the hard-bitten Madison Square Garden crowd.

Gretzky won more awards, set more records, scored more points, and dominated on offense more than any other player who ever competed. However, it was never just about the numbers. It was the joy, passion, and emotion that he played with every night that allowed him to reach those unscalable heights.

#3

Gordie Howe

Twenty-five seasons with Detroit Red Wings. Four years with Houston Aeros (WHA). Two years with New England Whalers (WHA). One year with Hartford Whalers.

New York Rangers fans are familiar with a certain chant they heard regularly from opposing fan bases—most notably the New York Islanders—for many years.

The sing-song "1940" chant mocked the Rangers' inability to win the Stanley Cup after that season, and they were not able to silence it until they finally won the title in 1994. However, they probably still hear that bit of mockery in their nightmares.

If history had been altered by just a degree, 1940 might just be one of several years that the Rangers won the Stanley Cup. That's because Gordie Howe had a tryout with the Rangers when he was fifteen years old.

Howe was a big, strong player at that age, and he went to the Rangers' training camp in Winnipeg to show what he could do against the best players in the world. Howe did not play like he would become one of the best players who ever played the game.

> **Career regular season:**
> NHL: 1,767 games, 801 goals, 1,049 assists, 1,850 points
> WHA: 419 games, 174 goals, 334 assists, 508 points
> Six-time Art Ross Trophy winner (Scoring Leader)
> Six-time Hart Trophy winner (MVP)
> One-time Gary L. Davidson Award/Gordie Howe Trophy winner (WHA MVP)
> 12-time first-team NHL All-Star; nine-time second-team NHL All-Star; two-time WHA first-team All-Star
> Four-time Stanley Cup winner
> Elected to Hall of Fame in 1972
> **Advanced stats: 186.6 OPS, 30.5 DPS, 217.1 PS (NHL only)**

Instead, he was just a homesick kid who was uncomfortable in that environment.

Just a year later, he went to camp with the Detroit Red Wings in Saskatchewan. He made a much better impression on the Red Wings, and by the time he was eighteen, he was playing regularly in the NHL.

The rest is history. Howe became a rock-hard right wing for the Red Wings who excelled in all areas of the game. He may never have been the best skater, shooter, passer, or stickhandler, but he was superb in all areas.

Nobody ever combined those skills to the extent that Howe did, and there has never been a superstar in any sport who competed at such a high level for so many years as Howe did.

Wayne Gretzky went on to break all of Howe's scoring records, and Bobby Orr certainly had more flash than Howe ever displayed, but don't think for a second that Howe's achievements are diminished.

He became known as "Mr. Hockey," and that's a title that neither Gretzky nor Orr would want to take from him. He also became known for his tough, physical play; subsequently, a player who scored a goal and an assist and also got into a fight in the same game was known for scoring a "Gordie Howe" hat trick.

Howe finished in the top five in scoring in the NHL for twenty consecutive years, and that's something that no other player can even get close to. Howe had ambidextrous skill. While he could fire off a brilliant backhander when he wanted to, he was equally good at taking a left-handed wrist shot as he was a right-handed one. That made it very difficult to defend Howe, because he was able to buy extra time and space because of that ability.

Howe did not start out as if he would become one of the sport's all-time iconic figures. He scored just seven goals and 15 assists as a rookie, but he made other contributions. He showed off his strength in puck battles and his ability to punish opponents with hard checks and nasty elbows. Players learned quickly not to challenge Howe, because of his explosive strength and punching power. One of those who learned the hard way was Montreal Canadiens superstar Maurice "The Rocket" Richard, who was knocked out cold in a one-punch fight with Howe.

Howe became a remarkable player in 1949–50, his fourth year in the NHL, after three ordinary seasons. He scored 35 goals and 33 assists, and he followed that with a career-defining year in 1950–51, when he dominated the league with 43 goals and 43 assists.

He followed that by scoring 47 goals in 1951–52 and 49 goals the following year. Both of those performances allowed him to stake his claim in the NHL as the league's best player. He won the Hart Trophy in both seasons, and he won the league scoring championship four years running from 1950–51 through 1953–54.

The Red Wings were becoming the dominant team in the NHL in the early 1950s, as they won four championships between 1950

Gordie Howe

and 1955. If any team was going to beat Detroit, it was going to have to get the best of Howe, and that was the most difficult task imaginable.

Howe escaped disaster during the 1950 playoffs. The Wings were engaged in a series with the Toronto Maple Leafs, and Howe tried to put his imprint on his rivals in the first game. Ted "Teeder" Kennedy had the puck for the Leafs and as he skated past center ice, Howe tried to run him over with a hard check. Kennedy avoided the onrushing freight train, and Howe steamrolled into the boards. Unconscious and bleeding, Howe was taken off the ice in a stretcher.

Emergency surgery to relieve pressure on his brain was performed, but it was not known if Howe would survive. He luckily made it through, and while he could not play the rest of the way, he showed up at the seventh game of the Stanley Cup Final against the Rangers, where the Leafs pulled out the victory.

Howe was a great team player throughout his career, which lasted from 1946–47 through 1979–80. He often deflected praise to his linemates, and during the glory years in the 1950s he played with Ted Lindsay and Sid Abel. That trio dominated the league's scoring leaders, finishing 1-2-3 in 1949–50.

Howe sustained his brilliance on a year-in, year-out basis and he had the highest scoring year of his career in 1968-69 when he scored 44 goals and 59 assists for the Red Wings at the age of forty.

Howe had a unique style that made it look like he was going for a skate in the park. However, he had remarkable strength in his legs and his ability to glide at full speed allowed him to win the race to the puck even when others looked like they were skating faster.

After the 1970–71 season, the forty-two-year-old Howe decided that arthritis in his left wrist was too painful to allow him to play at his best, and he retired from the Red Wings.

However, Howe came back and played with the Houston Aeros of the World Hockey Association in 1973–74. While his arthritic wrist felt somewhat better, Howe could not give up the chance to play pro hockey with his two sons Mark and Marty Howe.

Howe would play six seasons in the upstart league, and conclude his career at the age of fifty-one while playing for the Hartford Whalers in their first NHL season. Howe finally hung up his skates for good after his fifty-second birthday.

Howe was so good that he made 21 appearances on the NHL's first or second All-Star team, and another two on the WHA's first All-Star teams.

Throughout it all he remained the most humble of superstars, and he never uttered any words of braggadocio. However, those who are considered the sport's greatest never hesitate to remind the world of how great a player Howe was for so many years.

"He always was and always will be the greatest," said Gretzky, who made Howe his hero as a youngster.

Orr agreed with that assertion. "In my mind he's the best ever. Nobody will ever touch him. There have been a lot of great players in the past, and there will be a lot of great players in the future, but none will be as good as Gordie Howe."

#4

Mario Lemieux

Seventeen seasons with Pittsburgh Penguins.

Mario Lemieux always made it look easy—so easy, in fact, that it made teammates, coaches, and opponents shake their heads in awe when they saw him carry the puck up the ice with that glint in his eye.

Lemieux simply could do whatever he wanted on the ice nearly every time he laced up his skates. At 6-4 and 230 pounds, Lemieux could use his size to shield opponents from the puck when he established his position in the offensive zone. However, that was just a small part of Lemieux's game with the Pittsburgh Penguins.

Career regular season:
915 games, 690 goals, 1,033 assists, 1,723 points
Three Hart Trophies (MVP)
Six Art Ross Trophies (Leading Scorer)
Six-time NHL first-team All-Star, four-time second-team NHL All-Star

He was a brilliant skater who combined a powerful stride with superb quickness and change of direction. He had amazing stickhandling ability that allowed him to gain time and space in the neutral zone and in the offensive end. When Lemieux was playing his game, it often looked like a man had stepped on the ice to play with teenagers, because he was able to make the plays he wanted to and it appeared that even the best defensive players had no power to stop him.

This was apparent from Day One. When Lemieux was a rookie, he played his first game in the 1984–85 season against the Boston Bruins and their stellar defenseman Ray Bourque. As the puck came to Bourque at the point, Lemieux accelerated quickly and knocked the puck off of Bourque's stick and onto center ice.

Lemieux brought it to another gear, gathered in the puck, and make Bourque look as if he was standing still. Lemieux was under full control, made two quick moves and slipped the puck into the net with ease. Not a bad way to start a career.

Lemieux's arrival in the NHL had been highly anticipated, and while it came at a time that Wayne Gretzky was dominating the sport for the Edmonton Oilers, there was a belief that Lemieux was nearly as special as the Great One. Lemieux was bigger, stronger, and faster than Gretzky, and his creativity and talent were nearly at the same level.

His ability changed the course of hockey in Pittsburgh. The Penguins had joined the league in the 1967–68 expansion, and they had never been anything but an ordinary team that had to fight for survival. The Penguins had won three playoff series in their history prior to Lemieux's arrival, and they had never given any serious thought to making a run at the championship.

Mario Lemieux

However, by the time Lemieux was midway through his rookie season with the Penguins, the perception of the franchise had changed dramatically. Lemieux quickly showed he was a game-changing player on the level of Gretzky, Bobby Orr, and Guy Lafleur, and the Penguins knew he was capable of leading them to the Stanley Cup if they could surround him with a decent level of talent.

Lemieux made great statements every year with his play as the Pittsburgh front office tried to fill that order and bring in the type of complementary players who could help take the team to the promised land.

Lemieux scored an even 100 points as a rookie with 43 goals and 57 points, and that was his superb jumping-off point. He flexed his muscles and warmed up that rookie year, and then started carrying the Penguins on his back. He followed that rookie season with a 141-point effort in 1985–86 (48 goals and 93 assists), and came back the following year with 107 points (54 goals and 53 assists) in 63 games. Lemieux was limited that year by back problems, an issue that would flare up and trouble him at various points in his career.

As promising as Lemieux was in the NHL, he came into his own during the 1987 Canada Cup tournament. Playing on a team of All-Stars, Lemieux and Gretzky led Canada to the world championship of hockey as he scored 11 goals and seven assists in nine games. His 18 points were second to Gretzky's 21 points, and four of his goals were game-winners. While others already knew how good he was, the performance convinced Lemieux that he was one of the sport's elite players.

"I learned so much about how the great players work and conduct themselves," Lemieux said. "Remember, I was only twenty-one years old at the time. To be around guys like Wayne and Mark Messier and Paul Coffey, guys who'd already had so much success and had won Stanley Cups, was a tremendous learning experience."

Lemieux became the most dynamic player in the league. He scored an eye-catching and league-leading 168 points in 1987–88 (70 goals and 98 assists), and then scored an other-worldly 199 points the following season that included 85 goals and 114 assists. Lemieux once again led the league in scoring.

The Penguins picked up steam throughout Lemieux's career, and while he missed much of the 1990–91 season with back difficulties, the Penguins had built a powerful team that included Mark Recchi, Paul Coffey, Jaromir Jagr, Kevin Stevens, Joey Mullen, and goaltender Tom Barrasso.

Lemieux played just 25 regular-season games, but he scored 26 goals and 19 assists and he was approaching top form as the playoffs got underway. The Penguins struggled to get by the feisty New Jersey Devils in seven games, but they asserted themselves in the second round by defeating the Washington Capitals in five games.

That victory put them in the NHL's Eastern Conference Final against the Boston Bruins, and if they could win that series, they would play for the Stanley Cup. The Penguins looked fairly timid as they dropped the first two games of the series. However, when the series went to Pittsburgh for Game 3, the Penguins asserted themselves and let their talent take over. They went on to beat the Bruins in six games.

The Stanley Cup Final saw the Penguins take on the Minnesota North Stars, who had come into the league with the Penguins in the 1967–68 expansion and were also playing for the championship for the first time in their history.

The Penguins scored 28 goals in six games and rolled to the title. Their 8-0 victory in the final game of the series featured a goal and three assists by Lemieux.

He was the best player in the postseason, as he scored 16 goals and a league-best 44 points during the playoffs.

The Penguins would be an even stronger team the following season and they would defend their title. Lemieux scored 16 goals and 34 points in the postseason as the Penguins swept the Chicago Blackhawks in the Stanley Cup Final. Lemieux won the Conn Smythe Trophy as the playoff MVP.

Lemieux appeared to have the talent to challenge Gretzky as the era's greatest player. However, he did not have good health. In addition to his back problem, Lemieux suffered through a bout of Hodgkin's disease that slowed him down dramatically.

Lemieux started the 1992–93 season at the top of his game, and it looked like he might be able to challenge Gretzky's all-time scoring record of 215 points in one season. However, even though he was overpowering opponents on the ice, he had to step away from the game to battle cancer.

While he was able to return to action just a couple of months later and do it in spectacular fashion, the battle with Hodgkin's robbed him of his chance to set new NHL records.

Lemieux is the league's No. 2 point producer in points per game with an average of 1.883 points. He was just a fraction of a point behind Gretzky, who scored 1.923 points per night. Sniper Mike Bossy, perhaps the NHL's most accurate and best shooter, averaged 1.497 points per game and is third in that category.

Few players have ever been able to take over a game like Lemieux. He had more God-given natural talent than any player besides Orr. No player was better in one-on-one situations, and his elite ability allowed him to rise to the game's highest level.

#5

Mark Messier

Twelve seasons with Edmonton Oilers. Ten seasons with New York Rangers. Three seasons with Vancouver Canucks.

Leadership is a characteristic that is often overstated in sports, because analysts love to talk about this intangible quality and credit certain athletes with it when their team wins or puts on a stellar performance.

However, there are no statistics that measure leadership. What one teammate, coach, general manager, or sportswriter believes is leadership may vary from game to game or season to season. A player who comes through with a huge game when his team needs it is often cited as a great leader.

A true leader comes through regularly. He may have one or two signature performances along the way, but that leadership quality is there for teammates, opponents, coaches, fans, and media members to see on nearly an every-game basis.

A number of the greatest players of all-time had it. Maurice "The Rocket" Richard certainly had it. There was a singular look in his eye that became obvious in a game when his Montreal Canadiens were trailing or tied in the third period. That look said, "come on boys, time to get on my back."

Career regular season:
NHL: 1,756 games, 694 goals, 1,193 assists, 1,887 points
WHA: 52 games, 1 goal, 10 assists
One-time Conn Smythe Trophy winner (Playoff MVP)
Two-time Hart Trophy winner (MVP)
Two-time Ted Lindsay Award winner (Outstanding Offensive Player)
Four-time first-team NHL All-Star; one-time second-team NHL All-Star
Six-time Stanley Cup winner
Elected to Hall of Fame in 2007
Advanced stats: 135.6 OPS, 24.8 DPS, 160.5 PS

Bobby Orr, Jean Beliveau, Wayne Gretzky, and Gordie Howe all had that quality as well. But if there was ever a player that was able to give Richard a run for his money in that category, it was Mark Messier.

Playing the majority of his career with Gretzky, it would have been easy for Messier to get shunted to the background. Nobody, not even Messier, could score at the same rate as Gretzky. Messier may have scored 50 goals once in his career and 40 or more three times, but that's just peanuts compared to Gretzky's amazing numbers.

But Messier was so much more than a scorer. He was a hard-hitting and physical player. That did not necessarily mean he was going to get into fights, but he was going to make opponents earn every possession every time they went into the corner with him.

Messier battled for 200 feet every night. He was a brilliant skater and puck handler as he flew through the neutral zone, and he had a hard wrist shot and a nasty slapshot when he chose to wind up and blast.

When Messier was in the offensive zone, he basically lived in front of the net. While Gretzky's office was behind the goal line, where he operated with finesse, quickness, and subtlety, Messier was as subtle as a sledge hammer. When he went to the front of the net, he was going to establish his presence and he wasn't going to give up that position without a fight.

There was a fierceness to his game that is rarely seen among the most talented stars. Messier wanted to score, he wanted to win, and he wanted to punish opponents.

That's one of the reasons that playing the Oilers was such a tough assignment throughout the 1980s. Gretzky made it tough on his own with his unique ability to produce offense every time he stepped on the ice, and the Oilers also had other great talents like Jari Kurri and Paul Coffey. But Messier gave this team an incredible backbone.

He was as good in the defensive zone as any player that Glen Sather had on that dynamic team, and it made for a very long night for opponents.

While Gretzky's speed and quickness caused enough problems, Messier was able to bludgeon opponents with physical play and spectacular talent of his own.

Messier was a part of five championship teams with the Oilers. Four of those Stanley Cup titles came with Gretzky scoring at will, but the 1990 Oilers won the league title without the Great One. By that time, he had been traded to the Los Angeles Kings, and that made the Oilers Messier's team.

Messier had long proven his ability to play sensational hockey during the postseason. He had won the Conn Smythe Trophy during the 1984 playoffs when he scored eight goals and 18 assists, and he went on to score 10 goals or more in the playoffs on three different occasions.

Mark Messier

During the 1990 playoffs, few thought the Oilers were going to make a Stanley Cup run. They finished second in the Smythe Division to the Calgary Flames, and they had much to prove as the playoffs got underway.

They were pushed hard in the first round by the Winnipeg Jets before they put them away in the seventh game. A confrontation with Gretzky and the Kings came next, and the Oilers prevailed in a four-game sweep. They followed with a six-game Western Conference Final win before meeting the Presidents Trophy-winning Boston Bruins.

The Bruins had Ray Bourque and Cam Neely, and most favored them to win the series. But the Oilers won a triple overtime battle in Game 1 and won the series in five games. Messier was phenomenal, with nine goals and 22 assists in 22 games.

Messier was traded to the New York Rangers days before the start of the 1991 season, and most assumed that the main highlights of his career had already been seen during his glory days with the Oilers. However, Messier soon became the Rangers' fans' favorite player because of the verve and chutzpah he showed every night.

The Rangers were strong in the early 1990s, but it was Messier's presence that signaled a change in the team's fortunes.

New York had always seen its season end in heartbreak since 1940, which had been the last year the team had won the Stanley Cup. Everyone associated with the team had that fact rubbed in their collective faces every time the Rangers went to the Nassau Coliseum to play the neighboring New York Islanders. "1940" chanted the derisive Islanders fans in an effort to get under the Rangers' skin. They always succeeded.

But during the 1993–94 season, the Rangers had a brilliant team that finished first overall and was ready to rewrite history. With players like defenseman Brian Leetch and goalie Mike Richter, the Rangers were ready to end their 54-year Stanley Cup dryspell.

After sweeping the Islanders in four games and overpowering the Washington Caps in five, the Rangers met a strong New Jersey Devils team in the semifinals.

The Devils took a 3-2 lead after winning Game 5 at Madison Square Garden, and it looked like they were going home to New Jersey to clinch the series. However, that's when Messier's leadership took over. He knew his team was in a tough spot, but he told media members that the team would beat the Devils on their home ice and bring the series back to Madison Square Garden for a seventh game.

The Rangers were getting handled by the Devils in Game 6 and it looked like Messier would have to eat his words. However, he refused to lose, scoring three goals and adding an assist as New York roared to a 4-2 victory.

When Stephane Matteau scored in double overtime in Game 7, the Rangers had finally disposed of the Devils and they earned their chance to play the Vancouver Canucks in the Stanley Cup Final.

The Rangers played superbly in building a 3-1 lead, but the Canucks came back to win Games 5 and 6. The city of New York was on pins and needles as the Rangers prepared for the seventh game. Messier offered no guarantee in this game, but he scored a goal and an assist as the Rangers won the Stanley Cup with a 3-2 victory.

It was the crowning moment of Messier's career. Five Stanley Cups with the Oilers assured his status as one of the game's all-time great players, but one Stanley Cup with the Rangers helped propel him even further.

In a draft of the game's all-time greats, Orr, Gretzky, Howe, and Mario Lemieux might go before him. But the name of Messier would not go any further down the list, and he just might be the player that could carry his team to victory.

#6

Bobby Hull

Fifteen seasons with Chicago Blackhawks. Eight seasons with Winnipeg Jets (7 WHA, 1 NHL). One season with Hartford Whalers (NHL).

There are few images more iconic of the power, speed, and beauty of the NHL than the picture of Bobby Hull flying down the left wing for the Chicago Blackhawks as he crossed the blue line and wound up for the most devastating slapshot in the history of hockey.

There have been a few players who have been more effective than Hull—Bobby Orr, Wayne Gretzky, Mario Lemieux, Mark Messier and Gordie Howe—but perhaps no player had the ability

NHL: 1,063 games, 610 goals, 560 assists, 1,170 points
WHA: 411 games, 303 goals, 335 assists, 638 points
One-time Lady Byng winner (Gentlemanly Play)
Two-time Hart Trophy winner (MVP)
Three-time Art Ross Trophy winner (High Scorer)
Two-time Gary L. Davidson/ Gordie Howe Trophy winner (WHA MVP)
10-time first-team NHL All-Star; two-time second-team All-Star
Three-time first-team WHA All-Star; two-time WHA second-team All-Star
One-time Stanley Cup champion
Two-time Avco Cup champion (WHA league title)
Elected to Hall of Fame in 1983

to draw fans out of their seats and make them gasp with amazement like Hull when he was in full flight.

Hull had a powerful skating stride and an even more powerful shot. In the modern game, huge defenseman Zdeno Chara has often been recognized as having the hardest shot in hockey, and his slapshot has been timed at better than 108 miles per hour.

When Hull was in his prime with the Chicago Blackhawks, the NHL did not have the modern tools needed to measure the velocity as precisely as they do today. However, the rudimentary equipment used to measure shooting velocity basically confirmed what everyone in the league knew.

Hull had the hardest shot by a wide margin, and the speed of his shot was measured at 120 miles per hour. That may not have been precise, but it was clear that Hull's shot was a weapon to be feared.

Hull was an exciting teenage prospect when the Blackhawks brought him up to join the parent club in 1957–58. He showed he belonged right from the start, as he scored 47 and 50 points, respectively, in his first two seasons.

However, he became a star in his third season when he scored 39 goals and 42 assists to lead the league in scoring as a twenty-one-year-old.

Bobby Hull

In addition to winning the Art Ross Trophy, he finished second in the MVP voting and was named as a first-team All-Star.

More importantly, he was helping to lift the Blackhawks and enable them to become a powerful NHL team. He had plenty of assistance from Stan Mikita, and those two led the Blackhawks to a new level much the same way Jonathan Toews and Patrick Kane have done with the modern-day Blackhawks.

Chicago finished third in the regular season that year, but they got blitzed in the playoffs by the Montreal Canadiens, who eliminated them in four straight games.

The next year was a much different story. Once again they finished third in the regular season, but the team was brimming with confidence by the time the playoffs started. They had another matchup with the Canadiens, and this time the Blackhawks got the best of the Habs in six games.

They faced the Detroit Red Wings in the Stanley Cup Final, and they won the Stanley Cup by beating them in six games.

It appeared that the Blackhawks had a budding dynasty on their hands because the duo of Hull and Mikita were so young and talented. However, while they had several near misses, the Blackhawks would not win the Stanley Cup again during the Hull era.

But Hull drew fans to the Chicago Stadium and other arenas around the NHL because he had such a charismatic presence and immense physical gifts. Hull may have been just 5-foot-10 and 190 pounds, but he had rare strength that allowed him to outskate, outshoot, and outfight opponents when it came to puck possession.

If Hull engaged an opponent in a battle for the puck, he almost always came away with it. Hull became a goal-scoring machine for the Blackhawks, and he hit the 50-goal mark for the first time in his career in the 1961–62 season. Hull scored a record-breaking 54 goals in 1965–66 and followed up with 52 goals the next year, but those were just his warm-ups.

Hull took the goal-scoring record even further in 1968–69 when he blasted home 58 goals. The NHL's expansion in 1967–68 helped offensive players add to their scoring totals, but there was nothing cheap or flimsy about Hull's record. He had the best slapshot in the history of the game, he had a quick release on his wrist shot, and he was quite accurate with both.

Hull was never paid like a superstar when he was with the Blackhawks, and as the years passed, he grew quite resentful about it. When the World Hockey Association came into existence following the 1971–72 season, Winnipeg Jets owner Ben Hatskin made a strong sales-pitch to Hull, and offered him a 10-year, $2.75 million contract.

Hatskin had convinced the other WHA owners to pitch in to pay Hull's salary, saying that the superstar's presence would give the league credibility and convince other talented players to join the league.

Hatskin was right, but the primary beneficiary was the Jets, who would build a powerful team and win the WHA's first league championship. Hull would score 51 and 53 goals in his first two years in Winnipeg, but he would hit the heights in 1974–75 when he scored a remarkable 77 goals. That broke the major-league record set in 1970–71 of 76 goals that had been held by Phil Esposito of the Bruins.

Hull remained with the Jets through the WHA's final season in 1978–79. The Jets and three other WHA teams—the Hartford Whalers, Quebec Nordiques, and Edmonton Oilers—were all absorbed by the NHL after that season.

Hull played one more season, which he split between the Jets and Whalers. However, at the age of forty-one, he could no longer skate up and down the ice the way he could in his prime and he lost a few MPH off of his booming slapshot.

The one thing he truly wanted at the conclusion of his career was a rapprochement with the Blackhawks. He made his name and reputation while skating like a tornado and firing his bullet-like slapshot in front of the adoring fans at the Chicago Stadium.

His departure to Winnipeg caused a schism with Bill Wirtz, and that division would never get repaired during Wirtz's lifetime.

However, when Wirtz passed away in 2007, his son Rocky took over the franchise. Rocky knew that his father had a stubborn streak

Bobby Hull

that kept old grudges alive, and he was bound and determined to end them.

He welcomed Hull back to the team, and the Golden Jet became one of the team's treasured ambassadors.

He has a place with the Blackhawks, and he will always have a place in the annals of the game.

#7

Guy Lafleur

Fourteen seasons with Montreal Canadiens. Two seasons with Quebec Nordiques. One season with New York Rangers.

Guy LaFleur was far and away the best NHL prospect when the Montreal Canadiens drafted him with the No. 1 pick in the 1971 draft.

The fact that the Canadiens drafted him just a few weeks after winning the Stanley Cup with a stirring seven-game triumph over the Chicago Blackhawks doesn't make sense. The Habs should have been drafting last in the first round after celebrating their triumph.

Guy Lafleur

But, a fortuitous trade with the California Golden Seals had netted them the No. 1 pick.

Of all the brilliant moves made by Montreal general manager Sam Pollock during his career as the franchise's steward, this may have been the best.

Lafleur was not just another excellent player. He became a Montreal legend who finished his successful career in the same category as Rocket Richard, Jean Beliveau, Doug Harvey, and Jacques Plante.

> **Career regular season:**
> 1,126 games, 560 goals, 793 assists, 1,353 points
> Two-time Hart Trophy winner (MVP)
> Three-time Art Ross Trophy winner (High Scorer)
> One Conn Smythe Award winner (Playoff MVP)
> Three-time Ted Lindsay Award winner (Most Outstanding Player)
> Six-time first-team NHL All-Star
> Five-time Stanley Cup champion
> Elected to Hall of Fame in 1988

Beliveau retired at the conclusion of the 1971 championship run. As soon as the Habs drafted Lafleur, he offered to let "Le Demon Blond" have his revered No. 4 jersey. That's the number LaFleur wore as a junior superstar with the Quebec Remparts, but he realized that taking Beliveau's number would have been too huge of a burden.

Instead, he chose No. 10 and he created his own magical legacy. However, it took Lafleur a while to find his stride.

The first three years of his career were a relative struggle, as he scored 29, 28, and 21 goals. Those figures were relatively disappointing because Lafleur's pedigree meant that the scouts believed he would be a superstar from the outset of his career. While Lafleur would be part of a Stanley Cup-winning team in his second year, he didn't appear to play with the aggressiveness needed to take him to stardom.

As the word disappointment started to come into the conversation—at least at a whisper—Lafleur answered his critics in 1974-75. He scored 53 goals and 66 assists, and it marked the first of six consecutive seasons that he exceeded the 50-goal mark.

During his first three years, Lafleur was a bit surprised that it had been such a struggle for him. He expected to become a star right from the start. When that didn't happen, he began to squeeze his stick tighter and press harder.

But that changed in his fourth season. He regained the confidence he had that made him the No. 1 draft pick and he started to relax.

"I think it was always there and it was maybe a matter of bringing it out," Lafleur said about his talent and ability. "It was harder than I thought it would be and I had to try harder. I had to regain my confidence, maybe the most important thing. I have learned a lot to relax. I know what I can do now, and I do it."

Once the goals and the points started to pile up, Lafleur became one of the most dangerous players in the game. While he had some grit to his game, he also had remarkable speed, a blazing shot, and excellent playmaking ability.

However, there was one aspect of his game that was completely underrated. He had a remarkable ability to handle any pass that came his way and turn it into a scoring opportunity. It didn't have to be an accurate pass, either. If he got his stick on it, he found a way to control the puck and rip a vicious shot or make a pinpoint pass.

"That may have been what was most shocking about playing with Guy," said Hall of Famer and teammate Larry Robinson. "He always knew how to handle the puck and turn it into a scoring chance. He had these remarkable hands and instincts. It didn't have to be a perfect pass and many times they were bad ones. But Guy knew how to control the puck, get it onto the sweet spot of the stick, and then put it in the top corner. I never saw anybody else who could do that so well."

Lafleur became a first-team NHL all-star for six consecutive seasons, and he won the Hart Trophy in 1976-77 and 1977-78. He has scored more points (1,246) in Montreal Canadiens history than any other player, and he is second in goals (518) behind Richard.

The Canadiens reeled off four consecutive Stanley Cup championships when Lafleur was at his peak. They unseated the Philadelphia

Guy Lafleur

Flyers in four straight games in the Stanley Cup Final in '76, and then beat the Boston Bruins the following two years in the Finals as well.

The Bruins had one of the strongest teams of the decade in '77 and '78, but they had the misfortune of competing against the Habs when they were at their absolute peak. Montreal swept the Bruins in their first meeting, and then put them away in six games in '78. Many considered it a near miracle that the Bruins were able to extend the series to six games, because that's how talented the Lafleur-led Canadiens were.

The signature moment of Lafleur's brilliant career took place in the 1979 Stanley Cup semifinal round, where the Canadiens once again met Don Cherry's Bruins. This time, the two teams had split the first six games, and it appeared the Bruins might finally beat their ancient rivals when they took a 4-3 lead at the Montreal Forum with 3:59 to play in the third period.

But instead of killing the clock and advancing to the Stanley Cup Final, the Bruins were called for a too many men on the ice penalty at the worst time in the game. This meant that the Bruins had to try to defend Lafleur and the Canadiens' scintillating power play.

Lafleur started a rush from behind his own net, and quickly passed the puck to Jacques Lemaire. As the center made his way into the Boston zone, he left a drop pass for Lafleur. He hammered the puck with full force as it went just inside the far post about three or four inches off the ice for the tying goal.

"We had them, we finally had them," said Bruins defenseman Brad Park. "All we had to do was kill off a few minutes and we would have finally beaten them. But we got the penalty and Lafleur fires the shot heard around the world. It may have been the best shot ever taken."

Lafleur's streak of 50-goal seasons would finally come to an end in 1980-81. He would never score more than 30 goals again for the Habs and he would call it quits after the 1984-85 season.

However, Lafleur grew restless, and he returned in 1988-89 with the New York Rangers and then played two more years with the Quebec Nordiques before hanging up his skates for good.

By the way, he played those last three seasons after he had already been named to the Hall of Fame.

That's just one more way Lafleur broke the mold in the NHL.

#8

Ray Bourque

Twenty-two seasons with Boston Bruins. Two seasons with Colorado Avalanche.

You would be wrong if you said Bobby Orr was the leader in goals, assists, and points scored among Boston Bruins defensemen.

While there is little doubt that Orr was the greatest Bruins player, best NHL defenseman, and arguably the greatest player in the history of the sport, he did not have the gift of longevity. Injuries robbed him of a lengthy career.

Career regular season:
1,612 games, 410 goals, 1,169 assists, 1,579 points
Five-time Norris Trophy winner (Best Defenseman)
One-time Calder Trophy winner (Rookie of the Year)
One-time King Clancy Memorial Trophy winner (Leadership and Humanitarian)
Thirteen-time first-team NHL All-Star; six-time second-team NHL All-Star
One-time Stanley Cup champion
Elected to Hall of Fame in 2004

Ray Bourque did not have such a problem. He had a prolific career with the Boston Bruins, and when it looked like he would fall short of his lifelong goal of playing on a Stanley Cup-winning team, he was given that opportunity when the Bruins traded him in the late stages of his career to the talented Colorado Avalanche.

Bourque helped make that dream come true with some heroic performances in the 2001 Stanley Cup playoffs, but even if that had not happened, he might just rank as the second-best defenseman in the game's history.

An argument can be provided on behalf of Montreal great Doug Harvey and ancient Bruin Eddie Shore, but Bourque stands tall in their company.

Bourque was drafted by the Bruins with the eighth pick of the 1979 draft. That took place just a few weeks after the Bruins had suffered perhaps their most painful defeat, the "Too Many Men on the Ice" game against the Montreal Canadiens (see chapter seven).

That loss, authored by a late penalty that gave Guy Lafleur a chance to tie the game in the late stages on a blazing slapshot, which led to the winning goal in overtime, stopped an outstanding Bruins team from proceeding to the Stanley Cup Final.

The selection of Bourque was met with some hope, but few thought the Bruins had brought in a generational superstar.

However, when they saw him on the ice in training camp and throughout the 1979–80 season, that opinion quickly changed.

Ray Bourque

Bourque was an explosive offensive defenseman with a brilliant shot that featured eye-catching velocity and superb accuracy. He scored 17 goals from the blue line as a rookie, and he also added 48 assists. He was named a first-team NHL All-Star as a teenager, and that opening performance was no fluke. Bourque was named to the league's first or second All-Star team through the first seventeen years of his career.

Bourque was a do-it-all performer who realized that his first job was to prevent opponents from scoring. He did that in a number of ways, including with his hard-nosed physical play that allowed him to put his imprint on his opponents with his body checking, his superb skating ability, his shot-blocking skill, and his talent at anticipating what his opponents were going to do next.

While he was not as spectacular as Orr when he was skating with the puck, he was nearly as effective because he was so smart in the way he saw the game and so efficient with every movement on the ice.

Bruins president/general manager Harry Sinden was often asked to compare the two non-pareil defensemen. Sinden had served as one of the Bruins' head coaches during Orr's glory years with the Big, Bad Bruins and he was behind the bench when Orr scored his famous overtime goal against the St. Louis Blues in 1970 that gave the team its first Stanley Cup in twenty-nine years.

"It's not an easy decision," Sinden said. "But I would say if we were behind by a goal and needed to score, I would take Bobby. If we were protecting a one-goal lead late in the game, I would take Ray."

As strong as Bourque was from the start of his career, he improved as an offensive player during his first five years. He had a brilliant season in 1983-84, as he registered a career-high 31 goals and added 65 assists.

The Bruins were an excellent team throughout the majority of Bourque's run with them, and they got to the Stanley Cup Final in 1988 and 1990. The '88 team had beaten the Montreal Canadiens in the playoffs, and they were the first Bruins team to accomplish that feat since 1943.

With the burden of beating Montreal finally lifted, the Bruins defeated the New Jersey Devils in seven games in the Eastern

Conference Final and that gave them a date with the powerful Edmonton Oilers for the Stanley Cup.

The Bruins were wiped out in four games in Wayne Gretzky's last go-round with the Oilers. There was no shame in that loss, because the Oilers were nearly as dominant as the great Montreal Canadiens and New York Islanders dynasties that had preceded them.

The Bruins made it back to the Final two years later against Edmonton. While Gretzky had been traded to Los Angeles, the Oilers still had Mark Messier, Glenn Anderson, and a crew of brilliant players.

However, the 1990 Bruins were a tad better than the '88 team, and most thought the Bruins could give a much better account of themselves and possibly win the series.

The opener of the series was an NHL classic. The Oilers held a 2-1 lead late in the third period, but Bourque refused to let the Oilers hang on. He scored the tying goal on a blazing slapshot, and it was his second goal of the game.

That sent the game into overtime, and the two teams battled for extra periods. The Bruins nearly won in the second overtime when Glen Wesley had the puck on his backhand in front of a wide open net, but he fired it well over the inviting target and the Bruins missed their opportunity.

Edmonton reserve Petr Klima scored deep in the third overtime and the Bruins left the ice disheartened. They would lose the series in five games.

Bourque would continue to play outstanding hockey, but the Bruins would never get back to the Stanley Cup Final. As the years went by, Bourque requested a trade to a legitimate Stanley Cup contender.

Sinden made good on that request, and dealt him to the Avalanche before the 2000 trade deadline. While the Avs were beaten in the second round, Bourque knew the team was deep and talented. He decided to give it one more chance before he would retire.

The 2000-01 Avalanche had a dream season. They would dominate in the regular season and come away with the Presidents' Trophy after recording a 52-16-10-4 record for 118 points.

Ray Bourque

Bourque had been on great regular-season teams before, but none of them had won the Stanley Cup, and this would be his last chance.

The Avs rolled past the Vancouver Canucks in four games in the first round, but they were pushed to the limit before beating the Los Angeles Kings in seven games in the next. Bourque had two assists in that decisive seventh game.

Colorado took care of business in the Western Conference Final in five games, but the team had a huge obstacle in front of it if it was going to get Ray the Stanley Cup that he so desperately wanted. The New Jersey Devils had a brilliant team and goalie Martin Brodeur was one of the best puck stoppers in the game.

The Devils had a 3-2 lead with a chance to clinch the series in New Jersey in Game 6. However, Bourque refused to let his team lose. He had a brilliant defensive game and a plus-3 rating as the Avs recorded a 4-0 victory to send the series back to Denver.

The Avs played a tight, tough, and complete game and beat the Devils 3-1 to earn the title. Gary Bettman handed the Stanley Cup to captain Joe Sakic, and he quickly took three or four strides before he passed the great trophy to Bourque.

With tears streaming down his face and thunderous applause, he skated the Cup around the ice in Denver.

Bourque finally had his Stanley Cup and his fans in Colorado were thrilled, but no more so than his adoring public in Boston.

It was the most satisfying ending to a brilliant career.

#9

Stan Mikita

Twenty-two seasons with Chicago Blackhawks.

Generations of Chicago Blackhawks fans know the team has been led by some of the best centers who have played the game.

Jonathan Toews is the textbook example of how a center is supposed to play the game. He is a tough and responsible defensive player who ranks with the best in the game. He does an excellent job in the face-off circle. He is a top-flight offensive star who can score clutch goals and set up his teammates.

Stan Mikita

Prior to Toews, the Blackhawks had a brilliant star in Denis Savard, who was one of the most inventive players at the position. Magically talented and explosive, he never failed to bring the fans out of their seats.

But throughout the 1960s and '70s, Slovakian native Stan Mikita was Chicago's man in the middle. He teamed with dynamic Bobby Hull to make the Blackhawks perennial contenders, and Mikita often did the heavy lifting by playing on the power play, taking short-handed shifts, and playing his regular shift as the team's No. 1 center.

Career regular season:
1,394 games, 541 goals, 926 assists, 1,467 points
Two-time Hart Trophy winner (MVP)
Four-time Art Ross Trophy winner (Scoring)
Two-time Lady Byng Trophy winner (Gentlemanly Play)
Six-time first-team NHL All-Star; two-time second-team NHL All-Star
One-time Stanley Cup champion
Elected to Hall of Fame in 1983

Mikita got his chance to play with the Blackhawks as a nineteen-year-old in the 1959-60 season. He had actually played three games in the previous season, but the 5-foot-9, 152-pound Mikita played 67 games in 1959-60. Veteran Ted Lindsay, who was nearing the end of a brilliant career, was his left wing. Known as "Terrible Ted" because of his aggressiveness and vicious attitude on the ice despite a lack of size, he offered Mikita advice on how to stay in the NHL.

"You have to hit them first," Lindsay said. "They will try to run you out of the league if you let them. You have to go after them first."

Mikita, who went on to win the Lady Byng Trophy for gentlemanly play, took Lindsay's advice to heart. Mikita was not averse to getting into fights or using his stick as a point of emphasis. He exceeded the 100 penalty-minute mark in four of his first six seasons because he was not going to let bigger players run him out of the league.

While he was always willing to stand up for himself, Mikita also developed into a consistent and productive player who could both score and also set up his teammates. Mikita struggled throughout much of his rookie season with eight goals and 18 assists, but he became far more dependable in his second season in 1960-61 with 19 goals and 34 assists.

The Blackhawks also won the Stanley Cup that season, and it came so early in his career that Mikita thought that his team would get several more opportunities to lift the Stanley Cup. While they would get to the Stanley Cup Final on three more occasions during Mikita's career, the '61 Stanley Cup would be the only one that the Blackhawks won.

They defeated the Montreal Canadiens in six games in the first round and then took out the Detroit Red Wings in six games in the Stanley Cup Final.

Beating Montreal was the key moment for the Blackhawks, because the Habs had swept them in 1960 and defeated them in six games the year before that.

There was a determination in the Chicago locker room not to let the Canadiens have their way with the Hawks once again. Still, it was a very tall order because Montreal had finished in first place in the regular season with 92 points, 17 more than third-place Chicago.

It started badly, as Chicago rolled to a 6-2 victory in Game 1 at the Montreal Forum, but the Blackhawks bounced back with a 4-3 win in Game 2 to square the series.

The series moved to Chicago for the third game, and this turned out to be the one that gave the Blackhawks the confidence that they could stay with Montreal and beat them in the series.

Mikita called it the most memorable game of his career. The Black-hawks had a 1-0 lead late in the third period when Mikita and Bill Hicke engaged in a scrap that landed both men in the penalty box with two-minute roughing penalties. When they got to the penalty box, both men started swinging and the action resulted in five-minute fighting penalties and 10-minute misconduct penalties for both players.

Since there was less than seven minutes remaining in regulation, Mikita figured he was done for the night. However, Henri Richard tied the game for Montreal in the final minute, and Mikita was able to return shortly after the midway point of the first overtime.

Both teams hit multiple posts in the first two overtime periods, but the Blackhawks got a break when they were given a power play midway through the third overtime.

"I was playing the right point on the power play, but somehow I ended up on the left side," Mikita recalled. "The puck came out to me and I wound up to take a slapshot. I almost fanned on it, but I got enough on it to get it through the defense. It ended up on (teammate) Murray Balfour's stick and he wheeled around and sent it into the net for the win.

"They won the next game to tie the series, but it didn't matter. We knew we could beat them and we did."

The Blackhawks shut out the Habs in the last two games of the series and then took out the Red Wings in the Final.

There was heartbreak in losing Stanley Cup Finals to Toronto in 1962 and Montreal in 1965, 1971, and '73, but Mikita would become one of the most versatile and dynamic players in the league.

He also changed his game dramatically by the 1965–66 season. He didn't have to fight to survive any longer, and he admirably put that aspect of his game on the shelf. He also made a conscious decision to eliminate lazy penalties like hooking, holding, and tripping from his repertoire.

Mikita had already scored 30 or more goals twice in his career, and the 1965–66 season marked the start of a five-year streak in which he would top the 30-goal mark five straight times.

Mikita led the league in scoring in 1966–67, won the Hart Trophy, and also took home the Lady Byng Trophy. No player had ever recorded that hat trick before, and Mikita showed it was no fluke by repeating the feat the following year.

Mikita lasted twenty-two years in the NHL, and all of them were with the Blackhawks. In addition to his on-ice exploits, he was one of the first skaters to wear a protective helmet, and he is also given credit for helping to popularize the curved stick that allowed players to get more velocity and movement with their slapshots.

#10

Phil Esposito

Four seasons with Chicago Blackhawks. Nine seasons with Boston Bruins. Six seasons with New York Rangers.

The big center from Sault Ste. Marie, Ontario appeared to be on a path to a very solid career after the Chicago Blackhawks promoted him from the St. Louis Braves (Central Hockey League).

Phil Esposito fit right in with his teammates from the Windy City. Playing center on Bobby Hull's line meant that Esposito had one major job: He had to get the puck on a regular basis to the player with the hardest shot in the league.

Phil Esposito

Espo proved quite adept at that job, and he also showed he could score as well. He netted 23, 27, and 21 goals with the Blackhawks, and while he was not an All-Star, he showed he clearly belonged in the NHL.

While Espo was establishing himself, the Boston Bruins had taken notice of his growth. They had their own young superstar in Bobby Orr, and prior to the defenseman's second season, Boston management was committed to

Career regular season:
1,282 games, 717 goals, 873 assists, 1,590 points
Two-time Hart Trophy winner (MVP)
Two-time Ted Lindsay Award winner (Most Outstanding Player)
Five-time Art Ross Trophy winner (High Scorer)
Six-time first-team NHL All-Star; two-time second-team NHL All-Star
Elected to Hall of Fame in 1984
Advanced stats: 142.9 OPS, 20.9 DPS, 163.8 PS

getting talented offensive players who could take advantage of his speed, instincts, and playmaking skills.

Esposito was at the top of the Bruins' list, and after the 1966–67 season ended, Boston general manager Milt Schmidt made his move. He acquired Esposito, right wing Ken Hodge, and center Fred Stanfield for forward Pit Martin, defenseman Gilles Marotte, and goalie Jack Norris.

The trade was perhaps the most one-sided in the history of the four major North American sports. Stanfield became a productive player, Hodge eventually eclipsed the 50-goal mark, and Esposito became a record-breaking scorer and one of the game's all-time greats.

While the Blackhawks largely wanted Esposito to be a sharp passer and a set-up man for the explosive Hull, the Bruins wanted him to put the puck in the net.

He scored 35 goals and a league-leading 49 assists in his first season with the Bruins, and he earned second-team All-Star status.

He was just getting started and so were the Bruins. They made the playoffs that season, but the young team was eliminated in four games by the Montreal Canadiens.

However, that defeat did not set Orr, Esposito, & Co. back. They had gotten a taste of the postseason and the Bruins would be hungry for more.

The team was built around their incredible young defenseman and their big center. Esposito had a knack for establishing position in front of the net and he was able to handle the puck in traffic and create scoring opportunities. He could fire the puck with his forehand or backhand from the slot, jump on rebounds, or deflect shots into the net. He had always known he could score at the NHL level, and the Bruins were giving him that opportunity and asking him to run with it.

"It was the ideal situation," Esposito said. "The Bruins were a young and hungry team, and we were becoming a force. Bobby was already this incredible player and we needed scoring. I was going to do my best to score as much as I could, and they encouraged me to shoot whenever I had the opportunity."

The 1968–69 season was another step up the ladder for the Bruins and Esposito. They rolled to a 100-point season that was good for second place in the East Division behind the Canadiens. Esposito scored 49 goals and a league-record 126 points, and that earned him the Hart Trophy as the league's Most Valuable Player.

The Bruins swept the Toronto Maple Leafs in the playoffs, registering 10-0 and 7-0 victories in the first two games of the series. They met the Canadiens in the second round, and while they extended the Habs to six games, they still could not beat their ancient rivals.

Still, the Bruins knew they were knocking on the door of greatness. Esposito would score 43 goals and 99 points in 1969–70, which was a bit of a comedown from his record-setting performance the previous year. However, the Bruins were functioning as a finely tuned machine, and they would prove it in the postseason.

They defeated the New York Rangers in six hard-fought games, and then faced Espo's old team in the second round. Not only would the big center get a chance to play against the team that had traded

Phil Esposito

him, he would be fighting against his brother. Tony Esposito had enjoyed a dynamic season in net for Chicago and had registered 15 shutouts.

The two teams had finished tied for first in the Eastern Conference, but the Blackhawks had earned first place overall because they had more wins than the Bruins. The series was expected to be a tight one.

However, the Bruins solved Tony Esposito with ease, and it was his brother who did most of the damage. He attacked the Chicago net with his deadly snap shot, and beat brother Tony Esposito regularly.

The Bruins swept that series and the Stanley Cup Final against the St. Louis Blues as well. It was Boston's first Stanley Cup in twenty-nine seasons.

The Bruins were at their peak in the 1970–71 season, and Esposito was unstoppable. He had a magnificent year with 76 goals and 76 assists, and his 152 points would stand as an NHL record until Wayne Gretzky came along.

Esposito was so prolific that he inspired one of the greatest bumper stickers of all time. "Jesus Saves.... And Espo Scores on the Rebound" became a classic automobile adornment in the Boston metropolitan area.

The Bruins were not only scoring at a record rate—they netted 399 goals that year—they ran through the league with a cockiness rarely seen in professional sports. They regularly blew out the competition and a repeat performance in the Stanley Cup playoffs seemed to be certain.

But the overconfident Bruins met their match when they faced off against Montreal in the first round. Rookie Ken Dryden was an unknown in goal, but he slowed Boston's vaunted attack. A frustrated Esposito called the 6-foot-4 Dryden "a thieving giraffe," and the Habs shocked the Bruins in seven games.

The loss was humiliating to Esposito and his teammates, and they came back a more focused and mature team the next year. While they were not quite as high-scoring as they had been in '70-71, they were a bit better defensively and there would be no stopping them. They rolled to one-sided victories in the playoffs over the Maple Leafs and the Blues, and they met the Rangers in the Stanley Cup Final.

The Bruins had a 3–2 lead in the series and the sixth game was played at Madison Square Garden. The Bruins held a slim 1–0 lead in the third period, and Esposito helped put the game away by setting up two goals by Wayne Cashman. The Bruins earned their second Stanley Cup in three seasons, and that victory represented one of Espo's proudest moments.

Perhaps the most trying moment of his career came just a few months later when Canada and the Soviet Union squared off in the first international meeting between the two powers. Team Canada was heavily favored, but it won just one of the first four games of the series, and that left the nation in a state of shock. Few expected the Soviets to put more than token pressure on Canada.

Esposito and his teammates were booed by the home fans, but they took three of four in Russia and ultimately pulled out a huge triumph by a 4–3–1 margin. While Paul Henderson famously scored the winning goal, few players contributed more than Esposito, who was a dynamic force for Canada. Espo scored seven goals and six assists in the eight-game series.

The Bruins eventually traded Esposito to the Rangers in a trade for New York stars Jean Ratelle and Brad Park, in a deal that shocked the hockey world.

Esposito had been seen as the enemy in New York when he wore a Bruins uniform, but he quickly became a favorite for Rangers fans. New York never won the Stanley Cup with Espo, but he led them to the Finals in 1979, where they lost to the Canadiens.

Esposito retired after the 1980–81 season, and eventually became one of the founders of the expansion Tampa Bay Lightning. However, Esposito scoring from the slot for the Boston Bruins is one of the NHL's most enduring images.

#11

Denis Potvin

Fifteen seasons with New York Islanders.

There was an air of dread around the 1972–73 New York Islanders. They were a first-year expansion team, but that doesn't explain it. They were historically bad and did not resemble a major-league team.

The Islanders gave no indications that they would be able to turn things around relatively quickly, as they won only 12 of 78 games in that first season, and they regularly got blown out by the NHL's most ordinary teams. The Islanders gave up more than twice as many

Career regular season:
1,060 games, 310 goals, 742 assists, 1,052 points
One-time Calder Trophy winner (Rookie of the Year)
Three-time Norris Trophy winner (Best Defenseman)
Five-time first-team NHL All-Star; two-time second-team NHL All-Star
Four-time Stanley Cup champion
Elected to Hall of Fame in 1991
Advanced stats: 81.4 OPS, 79.4 DPS, 160.7 PS

goals as they scored (348-170) and they were quite putrid on both sides of the ice.

In short, their offensive skills were lacking, their skating was slow and indecisive, and the goaltending was leaky. Other than that, they were doing just fine.

But the depression of that first season gave way to hope less than a month after the Montreal Canadiens won the Stanley Cup that year. The Islanders had the first pick in the 1973 amateur draft, and while the class was rich with talent that included Bob Gainey, Rick Middleton, and Lanny McDonald, there was clearly only one direction to go.

The Islanders selected stalwart defenseman Denis Potvin. While Potvin was not quite Bobby Orr, he was that same kind of two-way defenseman who could dominate with his offensive skills and make all the plays needed on the defensive end.

Potvin didn't know much about the expansion Islanders, but upon getting drafted, he met with general manager Bill Torrey and head coach Al Arbour. Potvin's offensive skills gave him license to attack in the offensive zone, but Arbour made sure he took care of all of his defensive responsibilities.

Arbour had been a career defenseman in the NHL and he had been a traditional blueliner who was only interested in preventing goals. He did not try to make Potvin over in his own image, but he wanted his young prospect to give the proper respect to the defensive aspects of the game.

In short, it was a near perfect marriage. Potvin came into the NHL with excellent offensive skills and a somewhat underdeveloped defensive game. Arbour worked with him consistently to improve in that area and Potvin soon became one of the best defensemen in the league.

"In the hockey sense, Al Arbour, who was a career NHL defenseman, did not harness me and say, 'Don't play the offensive game' that I enjoyed so much, but he taught me about the responsibility of playing at both ends," Potvin said. "There were times when I played a little too offensively and he had to pull me back."

Potvin won the Calder Trophy in 1973–74, scoring 17 goals and 37 assists for the fledgling expansion team. He made some dreadful mistakes, including missing the team bus to Philadelphia and a subsequent game against the Philadelphia Flyers, but he was able to quickly put his youthful problems behind him and not make the same mistake twice.

He also got significantly better in each of his next two seasons, and raised his goal total to 21 in 1974–75 and an astounding 31 the next season.

The Islanders made the playoffs in '74-75, and they had a first-round matchup with the established New York Rangers. In those days, the NHL experimented with a two-of-three series in that opening round, and the Islanders shocked their Original Six neighbors when they won the third and final game of the series at Madison Square Garden.

That triggered a remarkable first year in the Stanley Cup playoffs. The Islanders faced off against the Pittsburgh Penguins in the second round, and they appeared ready to go meekly as they dropped the first three games of the series. However, they staged a huge rally and came back to become the second team in NHL history to battle back from an 0-3 deficit to win the series.

The Islanders faced the defending champion Philadelphia Flyers in the semifinals, and once again went down by a 3-0 margin. They rallied again and tied the series 3-3, but could not pull out another seventh game miracle.

But the Islanders had given notice that they were no longer an "expansion" team and that they could play with the toughest teams in the league.

The Islanders were improving each year, as Torrey proved to be masterful in assessing talent and bringing in winning players in the draft. At the same time, Arbour was the perfect coach to work with young and developing talent because he pushed them hard without ruining their confidence.

Potvin developed into an All-Star defenseman and became the team's captain. He would score 30 or more goals in three of his first six seasons, and his defensive play got better each season. While the Islanders went through some difficulties in ensuing playoff years, the team was becoming rock solid.

By the time the Canadiens' run of four straight Stanley Cups came to an end in 1979, Potvin and the Islanders were ready to take the next step. Potvin was at his best on the biggest stage. Potvin scored an overtime goal in Game 1 of the Stanley Cup Final at Philadelphia, and that gave the Islanders an edge that they would not relinquish.

While the Flyers rebounded and won Games 2 and 5 on their home ice, the Islanders won all of their games at the Nassau Coliseum to clinch the Stanley Cup in 1980. Their fans went into a frenzy when Bob Nystrom scored the Cup-clinching goal in overtime of Game 6.

"It was just a tremendous feeling to set winning the Stanley Cup as our goal and then to go out and achieve it," Potvin said. "It felt even better than we thought it would, and it made us bound and determined to keep winning with our group."

With stars like Mike Bossy, Bryan Trottier, Clark Gillies, and goalie Billy Smith, the Islanders had more than the will to keep winning. They had the kind of rare talent that could sustain championships.

They won three more titles in successive years to give them four consecutive Stanley Cups, which is just what Montreal had done before the Islanders started their run.

Potvin was right in the middle of it. He was an explosive scorer and a stalwart defensive player who was a dynamic force for fifteen years with the Islanders.

He helped take a woeful expansion team and turn them into a dynasty in the blink of an eye. He was a remarkable player who was among the best defensemen of his or any generation.

#12

Mike Bossy

Ten seasons with New York Islanders.

It just doesn't make sense. When it comes to Mike Bossy, there is little doubt that he was one of the greatest goal scorers in the history of the game. While his career in the NHL lasted just ten seasons, he scored 573 goals in those years with the New York Islanders.

Bossy was not a behemoth like Phil Esposito who would anchor himself in front of the net and score a large majority of his goals on short shots, rebounds, and deflections. He did not have that going for him. Nor was he a wizard when it came to stickhandling and

Career regular season:
752 games, 573 goals, 553 assists, 1,126 points
One-time Conn Smythe Trophy winner (Playoff MVP)
One-time Calder Trophy winner (Rookie of the Year)
Three-time Lady Byng Trophy winner (Gentlemanly Play)
Five-time NHL first-team All-Star, three-time second-team NHL All-Star
Four-time Stanley Cup champion
Advanced stats: 93.1 OPS, 17.8 DPS, 110.9 PS
Elected to Hall of Fame in 1991

creating plays. He was not in the Wayne Gretzky or Mario Lemieux category.

But when he had the puck on his stick in the offensive zone, there was probably a better chance the puck would end up in the back of the net when Bossy fired it than nearly any other player in the history of the league.

But here's what doesn't make sense. When Bossy was drafted by the New York Islanders with the No. 15 pick in the 1977 draft, he was not thought of as a player who could basically score at will and carry a team on his back when he got on a hot streak—which was most of the time.

Twelve NHL teams passed on Bossy in that draft, while the New York Rangers and Toronto Maple Leafs (with two picks each) passed on him twice.

Many scouts were leery about his future in the NHL because the 6-0, 186-pound Bossy was too timid to compete in the NHL. He often heard threats throughout his junior career with Laval National and he was not about to engage anyone in fisticuffs. That was just not his style.

But he did put the puck in the net, beginning with the 1973–74 season. He scored 70 or more goals four straight seasons at the junior level, and he did not need a "get-acquainted" period when he joined the Islanders and went to his first training camp with them.

Islanders coach Al Arbour liked what he saw from Bossy, and he immediately put him on a line with two other talented young players in Bryan Trottier and Clark Gillies. Trottier was the brilliant center who could do it all, and he excelled at setting up Bossy and Gillies. Bossy had a knack for always going to the right spot, and if he had a split second, he could get off his wrist shot, snap shot, or blinding slapshot.

During his rookie season, Bossy scored 53 goals and 91 points and was a runaway rookie of the year award winner. There were still some around the league that saw Bossy's production as something of a fluke, given his disdain for violence and nastiness in the NHL.

Bossy had no problems with hard checking and physical play and he understood that aspect of the game, but he despised the gutter aspects of the game and his position never changed throughout his career.

If he was brilliant as a rookie, he got even better as he moved along. He scored 69 goals in his second season before slumping to 51 goals in his third season. By that point, Bossy had become the best sniper in the league on a team that had just won its first Stanley Cup.

His signature moment came during the 1980–81 season when Bossy took aim at one of the game's great legends, Maurice "Rocket" Richard. Bossy, a Quebec native, knew that Richard had been the only player in NHL history to score 50 goals in 50 games when he did it during the 1944–45 season.

Bossy knew he was capable of matching Richard's productivity, and he got off to a brilliant start with 25 goals in 23 games. That made him the hottest topic in the league and opponents were not going to allow Bossy to skate with impunity and fire pucks at will. Shadow players were assigned to him on a regular basis, but nothing seemed to slow down the explosive right wing.

Bossy recorded six hat tricks by the time the Islanders reached their 36th game of the season. When he was asked if he wanted to beat Esposito's 1970–71 record of 76 goals in 78 games, Bossy explained that it was Richard's 50 goals in 50 games that motivated him.

While Bossy was chasing that mark, so was high-scoring Charlie Simmer of the Los Angeles Kings. Simmer, a powerful left wing, fell just short when he scored three goals in his 50th game, leaving him with 49 total.

That same night, Bossy was also playing his 50th game of the season as the Islanders met the Quebec Nordiques. While Bossy was motivated and the Nassau Coliseum crowd was pumped up and ready to explode if Bossy could find the back of the net, it did not appear to be his night. Instead of dominating play and firing his blistering shot, Bossy appeared to be a half-step behind the action throughout the game.

But with less than two minutes to go in the game, Bossy took a sweet pass from Trottier inside the face-off circle and drove the puck to the back of the net. The goal set off a wild celebration for Bossy's teammates and fans.

The Islanders went on to win four straight championships as the core of Trottier, Bossy, Gillies, defenseman Denis Potvin, and goalie Billy Smith was simply superb. Those Islanders may not have gotten quite the notoriety of the great Montreal Canadiens' dynasty that preceded them—the Habs won four straight titles from 1976 through 1979—but they may have been just as good.

Throughout his career, Bossy was an unstoppable force when it came to scoring goals. In his first nine seasons, he was amazingly consistent with his production. He never scored fewer than 51 goals and he exceeded the 60-goal mark four times in his career.

Bossy's greatness is probably best exemplified by his production in 1986–87, his final year in the league. Even though he was only thirty and could have been enjoying the peak years of his career, Bossy was slowed by brutal back pain that made every movement painful. He was limited to 63 games that season, and nearly all of them were devastating ordeals for him.

Nevertheless, he still managed to score 38 goals that season. A large majority of NHL players could only dream of scoring that many goals in their best season, but that's what Bossy was able to accomplish despite being nearly crippled by the pain he went through.

Bossy played in an era that included Wayne Gretzky, Marcel Dionne, and Guy Lafleur, and he was never viewed as the best player in the game. But he was a part of four championship teams and he was elected to the Hall of Fame in 1991.

He was one of the most brilliant scorers in the history of the game, and there's no telling where his numbers would be if a bad back hadn't put a halt to his productivity.

#13

Patrick Roy

Twelve seasons with Montreal Canadiens. Eight seasons with Colorado Avalanche.

Patrick Roy is almost always in the conversation when it comes to ranking the best goaltenders of all-time. His unique style and quirky mannerisms gave him a distinct style, but whether he was leading the Montreal Canadiens or the Colorado Avalanche, Roy was the kind of goalie who gave his team a chance to win every night.

Patrick Roy

That's because he battled for 60 minutes, and if his team was overmatched, he still left it all on the ice and would throw his body around in an attempt to keep the puck out of the net. He was successful nearly every time.

Few thought that Roy would ever develop into a superstar goalie when the Canadiens selected him in the third round of the 1984 draft. There was hope that he would develop into a competent NHL goalie, but what he

Career regular season:
NHL Career: 1,029 games, 551-315-131, 2.54 goals-against average, .910 save percentage, 66 shutouts
Three-time Vezina Trophy winner (Top Goaltender)
Three-time Conn Smythe Trophy winner (Playoffs MVP)
Five-time William Jennings Trophy winner (Fewest Goals Allowed)
Four-time first-team NHL All-Star; Two-time second-team NHL All-Star
Four-time Stanley Cup winner
Elected to Hall of Fame in 2006

ultimately became—a superstar who would be compared with the greats in the game including Ken Dryden, Martin Brodeur, and Dominik Hasek—seemed more than a bit far-fetched.

Growing up in Quebec, Roy was a big fan of the Quebec Nordiques and had a hatred for the Canadiens in his blood. However, he quickly put all childhood loyalties aside as he led the Canadiens' minor-league team in Sherbrooke to the Calder Cup (emblematic of minor league supremacy) in 1984–85.

That showing earned Roy the chance to play for a good but not great Canadiens team in 1985–86. Montreal finished slightly better than .500 with a 40-33-7 record that left them in second place in the Adams Division behind the Nordiques. The Philadelphia Flyers and Washington Capitals, with 110 and 107 points respectively, had been the two best teams in the Eastern Conference, and it was expected that one of those teams would represent the Eastern Conference in the Stanley Cup Final.

Apparently, Roy did not get the memo. He had performed decently during his rookie season with a 3.35 goals-against average and an .875 save percentage. However, there was no indication that he would raise his play to another level in the postseason.

However, that's just what he did as the Canadiens started to roll. The Habs tormented the Boston Bruins in the first round and swept them in a best-of-five series. In the next round, the Hartford Whalers nearly outplayed Montreal, but Roy helped them survive in seven games.

The New York Rangers had beaten the favored Flyers and Capitals, and Montreal was going to have to get past the streaking Rangers if they wanted to make it to the Stanley Cup Final. Roy was at his best, as the Habs won the series in five games.

Calgary had managed to upset Wayne Gretzky and the Edmonton Oilers in the second round in seven games and the Flames followed that up with a seven-game triumph over the St. Louis Blues. They had raised their profile dramatically with the win over the explosive Oilers, and they were heavily favored to win their first Stanley Cup.

However, Roy and his teammates were simply sharper and more opportunistic and they won the series in five games. Roy was so good that he captured the Conn Smythe Trophy. He had registered a 15-5 record during the postseason with a shocking 1.92 GAA and a .923 save percentage.

Roy served notice just how special a goaltender he would be throughout his career with his remarkable playoff showing, and he went on to win the Vezina Trophy as the league's best goaltender three times with the Canadiens.

He led them back to the Stanley Cup Final again in 1989, where they once again faced the Calgary Flames. This time, the Flames and Canadiens had appeared to be on a collision course, since they had the two best records during the regular season by a wide margin. Many gave the edge to the Canadiens because of Roy's superiority in the net. He had a 2.09 GAA that season and he had a .908 save percentage.

Montreal rolled past Hartford, Boston, and Philadelphia in the Eastern Conference, while the Flames had beaten Vancouver, Los

Patrick Roy

Angeles, and Chicago in the Western Conference. When the Canadiens took a 2-1 lead after winning Game 3 in double overtime on a goal by Ryan Walter, it looked like that championship was about to return to Montreal once again.

However, the Flames got superb play from goalie Mike Vernon, Joey Mullen, Doug Gilmour, and the mustachioed Lanny McDonald the rest of the way and won the title in six games.

The defeat was a bitter one for Roy, and he had to wait four long years to get back to the Stanley Cup Final. The Habs recorded 102 points that year, but it was good for just third place in the Adams Division.

However, they were quite remarkable in the playoffs. After dropping the first two games at home to the Quebec Nordiques in the opening round, the Canadiens bounced back and won the series in six games.

They followed with easy victories over the Buffalo Sabres and New York Islanders, and that earned them a spot in the Stanley Cup Final against Wayne Gretzky and the suddenly explosive Los Angeles Kings.

After the Kings won the first game at the Montreal Forum, the Habs trailed Game 2 by a 2-1 margin late in the third period when Montreal head coach Jacques Demers called for a stick measurement on Kings forward Marty McSorley. The stick had too much of a curve and the Kings were penalized. Eric Desjardins of the Canadiens scored on the subsequent power play to tie the score and he won the game on a goal in overtime.

Overtime victories became the theme of the Habs' 1993 playoff run, as they reeled off 10 straight extra time wins after losing to Quebec in overtime in the first round. They followed their Game 2 win with two more OT victories in Los Angeles, before returning home to close out the series in five games as their adoring fans cheered and wept. Roy picked up his second Conn Smythe Trophy after going 16-4 with a 2.13 GAA and a .929 save percentage.

The Canadiens have not won a Stanley Cup since then.

The end of Roy's career with the Habs would come slightly more than a year later. He was clashing regularly with head coach Mario Tremblay during the 1994–95 season, and when Tremblay left Roy in goal in a rout at home against the Detroit Red Wings, Roy had had enough.

After giving up nine goals before finally getting pulled, an angry Roy told Tremblay and the general manager that he would never play for the Canadiens again because he felt the team had embarrassed him.

Roy worked out a trade with the Colorado Avalanche, with whom he excelled. He led them to two Stanley Cups, and he went on to win the Conn Smythe Trophy after the team won the 2001 title.

That was just a memorable run for Roy and his Avalanche teammate Ray Bourque. Roy was 16-6 in those playoffs with a 1.70 GAA, a .934 save percentage and a career-best four playoff shutouts. Roy and the Avalanche not only wanted to win for themselves, but also for Bourque, who had enjoyed a brilliant career with the Boston Bruins but never got to lift the Cup with them.

He had come to the Avs in 2000, and it was fairly clear that the 2000-01 season was going to be his last. Roy, Joe Sakic, and Peter Forsberg made it clear that they wanted to get Bourque his championship and they succeeded with a seven-game triumph over the New Jersey Devils.

The bond between Roy and Bourque was especially poignant, because they had been rivals for so many years when Roy played for Montreal and Bourque starred for the Bruins.

Roy was inducted into the Hall of Fame in 2006, and it was an emotional time for him. "It means a lot, it's the crowning achievement of my career," Roy said. "There were a lot of good moments, but having the chance to be part of the Hockey Hall of Fame is something that I never thought would be possible. It means a lot to me."

He may have never thought he could get there, but he was perhaps the best money goalie in the history of the game.

#14

Jean Beliveau

Twenty seasons with Montreal Canadiens.

In the minds of many sports fans, the life of a professional athlete is a gift, and therefore those that have the talent to play in the NHL should feel grateful.

It doesn't always work that way. Those who skate faster or shoot harder than everyone else often find their talent acknowledged at an early age. Instead of feeling thrilled or proud, some may start to feel entitled because they regularly hear how great they are.

Career regular season:
1,125 games, 507 goals, 712 assists, 1,219 points
Two-time Hart Trophy winner (MVP)
One-time Ross Trophy winner (Leading Scorer)
One-time Conn Smythe Trophy winner (Playoff MVP)
Five-time first-team NHL All-Star; Four-time second-team NHL All-Star
Ten-time Stanley Cup winner
Elected to Hall of Fame in 1972
Advanced stats: 116.8 OPS, 21.3 DPS, 138.1 PS

They become spoiled and self-righteous, and difficult to be around.

But then there are others who keep themselves and their careers in perspective. They know how lucky they are to be paid huge sums of money to play a game they yearned for as children. They may accomplish much, but still they remain decent and humble.

There was no hockey player—and no athlete in any sport—who followed that example better than Jean Beliveau of the Montreal Canadiens.

There may have been a very few hockey players who were better than Beliveau—perhaps Bobby Orr, Wayne Gretzky, and Gordie Howe—but there was never a player before or since who carried himself with more pride and dignity than Beliveau.

You can find many stories that indicate the superb and selfless manner in which Beliveau lived his life. He retired from the Canadiens in 1971, but he always remained at the forefront of the sport. He dedicated much of his time and effort to helping others, and he did it with kindness and warmth.

What made Beliveau such a great person is that he conducted himself with dignity and respect in everything he did, yet there was not a trace of arrogance to him. He was hockey royalty, but he refused to fall into the trap of celebrity superiority—not even a trace, not even once.

His career was one of brilliance for the great Montreal Canadiens. He scored 507 goals and 1,219 points during his run in the NHL

Jean Beliveau

from 1950–51 through 1970–71. Actually, his first full season in the NHL was 1953–54, and from that point forward he was always a brilliant performer.

Consider his final season at the age of thirty-nine. He scored 76 points in 70 games, and while the Canadiens were expected to get knocked out of the playoffs in the first round by the Big, Bad Boston Bruins, Beliveau and the Habs not only defeated Boston but went on to win the Stanley Cup.

Beliveau scored six goals and 16 assists during that Stanley Cup run, and his last game in the NHL came at the venerable Chicago Stadium, where he got to skate around with the Stanley Cup for the tenth time as a player.

He was strong, healthy, and in good shape, and could have played longer if he wanted. The World Hockey Association's Quebec Nordiques tried to tempt him out of retirement with a contract that would have paid him more than he made during his entire career with the Canadiens, but he never budged. Beliveau did not play the game for riches. He wanted to be at his best; he was not going to put on another uniform if he did not think he was going to be at his best.

"I made up my mind to offer my place to a younger player," Beliveau said. "It's hard, but I will play no more. I only hope that I have made a contribution to a great game. Hockey has been my life since the day my father gave me a pair of skates when I was five years old."

If Beliveau held on to his principles at the end of his career, he held them just as tightly at the beginning.

When Beliveau was coming of age as a hockey-playing phenom in the late 1940s in Quebec, the Montreal Canadiens bought the Quebec Senior Hockey League he was playing in, just so they could get his rights and he could eventually play for them.

However, Beliveau was in no hurry to join the Habs, because he was treated so well by the Quebec Aces and because he enjoyed playing at home. However, he finally relented and joined the Canadiens for the 1953–54 season.

Beliveau quickly showed off his talent and he was a superstar by the 1954–55 season when he scored 37 goals and 36 assists. The

Canadiens beat the Boston Bruins in the opening round of the playoffs, but they fell to the Detroit Red Wings in seven games with the title on the line. Beliveau had been magnificent, with six goals and seven assists in 12 games.

That would be the last series loss the Canadiens suffered until 1961. Montreal won five straight Stanley Cups, and Beliveau was often at the forefront of the heroics. He scored a league-best 12 goals and seven assists in the 1956 championship run, and he averaged better than 1.2 points per game while playing 41 Stanley Cup games over that five-year period.

That Montreal dynasty is often looked at as one of the greatest teams of all-time.

By the time Beliveau and the Habs won their next Stanley Cup in 1965, Beliveau was a savvy veteran of thirty-three years old. He may not have been as quick as he had been in his early years, but he more than made up for it with the savvy level of play that he had gained in so many Stanley Cup runs.

Beliveau and the Habs would win championships in five of his last six seasons.

After his career was over, Beliveau would remain with the Habs in their front office and later as an ambassador for the team.

There could be no better representative for the team or the sport. His mission as a hockey player was to help the Canadiens win championships. His mission in life was to always give back and give people he came in contact with a chance to improve themselves.

He succeeded at both in spectacular fashion. When he passed away in December 2014, thousands filed past his coffin in tribute to the brilliant hockey player and even better human being.

#15

Steve Yzerman

Twenty-two seasons with Detroit Red Wings.

If the Detroit Red Wings had gotten their man in the 1983 amateur draft, Steve Yzerman never would have been part of the team.

The Red Wings had the No. 4 pick in the draft, and they were hoping to select hometown hero Pat LaFontaine. At the time, the Red Wings were a struggling team who were hoping to rebuild their fan base and play respectable hockey. A youngster from the Detroit area who had been a star on the international stage like LaFontaine would certainly have given them a great chance to do just that.

Career regular season:
1,514 games, 692 goals, 1,063 assists, 1,755 points
One-time Ted Lindsay Trophy winner (Outstanding Offensive Player)
One-time Conn Smythe Trophy winner (Playoff MVP)
One-time Frank J. Selke Trophy winner (Best Defensive Forward)
One-time Bill Masterton Trophy (Perseverance and Sportsmanship)
One-time first-team NHL All-Star
Three-time Stanley Cup champion
Elected to Hall of Fame in 2009
Advanced stats: 139.4 OPS, 27.2 DPS, 166.7 PS

But the Red Wings never had a chance to pick LaFontaine, as the Buffalo Sabres beat them to it.

That move is perhaps the best disappointment the Red Wings ever had. They may not have gotten the local hero, but they selected Steve Yzerman with the No. 4 pick, and he is clearly one of the top four players to ever compete for the franchise.

Gordie Howe is No. 1, and you can put Yzerman, Nicklas Lidstrom, and Ted Lindsay together and divide them any way you want. That's how good Yzerman was for the Red Wings in his twenty-two-year career in Motown.

Yzerman wasted no time showing the Red Wings and their long-suffering fans that he was going to help turn around their fortunes. He scored 39 goals and 48 assists in his rookie season of 1983–84, and he was second in the NHL's Calder Trophy voting to goalie Tom Barrasso of the Sabres.

He made an impression in the first game he ever played. Yzerman scored a goal and an assist in a trip to Winnipeg, and it showed Yzerman that he could play in the NHL, even though he was shaking with anxiety when he took the ice.

"I was nervous because I didn't know what to expect and my dad was in town," Yzerman said. "Then, I remember being comfortable with how I was doing with the pace. It was a pleasant surprise."

Steve Yzerman

More importantly, the Red Wings made the playoffs that year, and that started a turnaround for the franchise. The Red Wings made the playoffs in Yzerman's first two seasons with the team. They faltered in 1985–86, but returned to postseason play in 1986–87. They missed the postseason again in 1989–90, but they would not falter after that. They made it every season from 1990–91 through the end of Yzerman's career in 2005–06, and they have continued to make the playoffs in every season since, a streak that has stayed alive through the end of the 2014–15 season.

Much of that was due to the tone that Yzerman set throughout his career. He was a dynamic offensive player from the start, but he was never satisfied just by scoring goals and making plays in the offensive zone. He was a solid 200-foot player who was outstanding in the face-off circle and he was also a very effective defensive player.

General manager Jimmy Devellano knew that Yzerman was special when the Red Wings drafted him, and he exceeded expectations in his first two years. He was so strong and responsible that the Red Wings named him captain in his third season, as just a twenty-one-year-old player.

Yzerman topped the 30-goal mark in three of his first four seasons with the Red Wings, but he blossomed during the 1987–88 season, when he scored 50 goals and added 52 assists. That began a streak of six consecutive seasons in which he scored 100 points or more.

He was at his best in the 1988–89 season, as he registered a franchise-best 155 points with 65 goals and 90 assists. That was a remarkable season by any standards, but Yzerman could only finish third in the Hart Trophy voting behind Wayne Gretzky and Mario Lemieux. Both of those all-time greats had remarkable seasons—Gretzky scored 54 goals and had 114 assists, while Lemieux was even more productive and prolific with 85 goals and 114 assists.

Suffice it to say that Yzerman had the best third-place finish in the history of the league's MVP voting.

The Red Wings were not yet a dominant team, but they would show signs of getting there in the 1991–92 season when they won the Norris Division and defeated the Minnesota North Stars in seven tough games in the playoffs. The Red Wings showed the heart of the champions they would eventually become as they rallied to win the series after falling behind three games to one.

They got swept by the Blackhawks in the next round, but the Red Wings were starting to learn what it was like to compete in the playoffs and win games at the most important time of the year.

They suffered a painful seven-game loss at the hands of the San Jose Sharks in 1993–94, and that defeat hardened the team. "We knew we let an opportunity slip through our grasp when we lost to San Jose," Yzerman said. "We knew we were the better team, but we didn't finish the way we needed to in that series. That pain stayed with us a long time."

The next year, the Red Wings beat the Dallas Stars in four games, and that gave them another shot at the Sharks. Detroit swept the series in four games and then defeated the Chicago Blackhawks in five games. That put the Red Wings in the Stanley Cup Final against the New Jersey Devils, and the Red Wings were swept in the series.

Yzerman would have one of his greatest individual moments in the 1995–96 playoffs. After the Red Wings beat the Winnipeg Jets in six games in the first round, the next series went to seven games against the St. Louis Blues.

Jon Casey of the Blues and Chris Osgood of the Red Wings kept that Game 7 scoreless into the second overtime. At that point, Yzerman cruised over the blue line with the puck and unleashed a brilliant slapshot just inside the top corner of the net. That goal set off a celebration in Detroit.

While they wouldn't win the Stanley Cup that year, they would in the 1996–97 season. The Red Wings got past the Avalanche in six games in the Western Conference Final and swept the Philadelphia Flyers in the Final for the franchise's first title in forty-two years.

That was the first of three Stanley Cups Yzerman would win with the Red Wings, and the second would come the next year when the Red Wings swept the Washington Capitals in four games.

Steve Yzerman

Yzerman had six goals and 18 assists in that playoff season and would earn the Conn Smythe Trophy as the playoff MVP.

It was the kind of special and consistent performance that would mark Yzerman's career. He had set the bar at a very high level from a very early moment, and he kept delivering throughout his long and memorable run with the Red Wings.

#16

Sidney Crosby
(through 2014–15)

Ten seasons with Pittsburgh Penguins.

If Wayne Gretzky was The Great One throughout his remarkable and record-setting career, Sidney Crosby was "The Next One" as he rose through Canada's amateur and junior ranks and he prepared for a career in the National Hockey League.

Crosby was drafted as a seventeen-year-old by the Pittsburgh Penguins in June of 2005. The hype had been incredible for Sid the Kid as he

Sidney Crosby (through 2014–15)

developed at Shattuck-St. Mary's in Minnesota and for Rimouski of the Quebec Major Junior Hockey League.

There was no doubt that Crosby was going to garner the top choice in the draft, although there was some grumbling that he would fall to the Penguins. Pittsburgh had been blessed with Mario Lemieux, who was the No. 2 player of his era behind Gretzky and possibly could have challenged Gretzky for the No. 1 slot if he had

Career regular season:
NHL: 627 games, 302 goals, 551 assists, 853 points.
Two-time Art Ross winner (Leading Scorer)
Two-time Hart Trophy winner (MVP)
Three-time Ted Lindsay Award winner (Most Outstanding Player)
Four-time first-team NHL All-Star; one-time second-team NHL All-Star
One-time Maurice Richard Trophy winner (Leading Goal Scorer)
One-time Stanley Cup winner
Advanced stats: 85.9 OPS, 19.1 DPS, 105.1 PS

been blessed with better health. Now the Penguins were also getting Crosby.

However, the hype and subsequent pressure on Crosby was tremendous. There were no guarantees that his tremendous skill levels would help him become the best player at the NHL level as he had been for his age group.

Veteran players don't take kindly to youngsters who are anointed with greatness even before they take their first step on the ice, and that was just what was happening with Crosby.

Crosby was a target for opposing defensemen and forwards from the minute he stepped on the ice and he was also burdened by huge expectations. However, instead of being weighed down by both factors, Crosby showed off his superstar talent from the start.

Crosby scored at an eye-opening rate as a rookie for the Penguins, recording 39 goals and 63 assists as he exceeded the 100-point mark as a rookie. He became the Penguins' No. 1 scoring option and helped give the Penguins an identity.

The Penguins did not make the playoffs during the 2005–06 season and their record indicated they were no better than they had been the previous season, as they ended the year with 58 points in both seasons. However, Crosby was a presence on the ice that year, and he learned the ropes as a rookie; the future seemed unlimited.

It should be noted that the much-hyped Crosby did not win the Calder Trophy as the league's best rookie. That honor went to Alex Ovechkin of the Washington Capitals. The powerful Russian forward had come into the league as the No. 1 pick in the 1984 draft because of his big shot and drive in the offensive zone. He exceeded expectations with 52 goals and 54 assists, and he edged out Crosby for the Calder Trophy.

Crosby and Ovechkin would develop an intense personal rivalry because of their all-around status as well as their importance to the sport. Additionally, they had divergent personalities as Crosby was humble and private, while Ovechkin was loud and enjoyed the spotlight.

Crosby's game developed at a dramatic level the next season. He became the league's best offensive player, scoring 36 goals and 84 assists as he led the NHL in scoring and also earned the Hart Trophy as the Most Valuable Player. Crosby's value as a scorer was accelerated because of his pinpoint passes and his ability to put his shot wherever he wanted.

Crosby's ability to put the puck wherever he wanted seemed to rival that of Gretzky and Lemieux. While his point totals were not quite as high as that of those two players, much of that was due to the difference in the style of play during the eras in which these great players competed. Gretzky and Lemieux played in a wide-open era and didn't have to contend with the punishing physical hitting that Crosby often had to absorb.

The Penguins made the playoffs that year, but they were eliminated by the Ottawa Senators in the first round.

The next season would be a much different story. Crosby was named captain of the Penguins prior to the start of the season, and his great expectations for another spectacular scoring season were put on hold after he suffered a high ankle sprain that kept him out of 29 games. However, he still finished with 24 goals and 48 assists, and the Penguins (with 102 points) were the No. 2 team in the Eastern Conference behind the Montreal Canadiens.

Pittsburgh was prepared for a much better showing in the playoffs than it had been the year before. Crosby was chomping at the bit to show off his talents, and the Penguins roared through the Eastern Conference.

They got revenge on the Senators for the previous year's defeat by sweeping them in four games, and then beat the Rangers in five games to set up an Eastern Conference Final showdown with the Philadelphia Flyers. The Pens scored another five-game victory.

Crosby had been the key to the Penguins' superb postseason showing—he was dominant with six goals and 21 assists. While the Penguins were stopped in the Stanley Cup Final by the Detroit Red Wings in six games, the arrow for both Crosby and his team was pointing up.

The loss in the Stanley Cup Final had lit the fuse for a championship. Crosby and his teammates were quite formidable. Evgeni Malkin had joined Crosby on the Penguins and was a remarkable talent as well, leading the Penguins with 113 points, and Kris Letang was an exciting defenseman.

They also got game-changing goaltending from Marc-Andre Fleury. While he would have a slew of postseason difficulties later in his career, his play during the 2009 postseason gave the Penguins a big edge.

Crosby had scored 103 points during the regular season, but he was utterly spectacular in the playoffs, with 15 goals and 16 assists. Pittsburgh beat Philadelphia, Washington (and Ovechkin), and Carolina to get back to the Stanley Cup Final, and this time they got the best of Detroit, beating the Red Wings in seven games, including a road win in the last game.

Crosby then added to his reputation as he led Canada to the Olympic Hockey Gold Medal in the 2010 Winter Games in Vancouver.

Crosby scored the game-winning goal in overtime in a classic match against the United States that made him a full-fledged national hero.

Once he got back to the NHL, many thought that the victory against the Red Wings could be the first of many Stanley Cups for Crosby and the Penguins, because they seemed to be the most talented and driven team in the league.

However, they suffered a second-round upset at the hands of the Montreal Canadiens in 2010, and Crosby endured a brutal concussion that kept him out of the second half of the 2010–11 season and for nearly 75 percent of the 2011–12 season.

The 2012–13 season was torn apart by a lockout. Although Crosby was relatively healthy that season and scored 15 goals and 41 assists in 36 games—good enough to land him first-team All-Star status—he was not quite back to pre-injury levels.

That was demonstrated by the Penguins performance in the Eastern Conference Final against the Boston Bruins. Not only were the Penguins swept in four games, but they scored just two goals in four games.

Disappointing performances followed in the 2014 and 2015 playoffs, although Crosby once again topped the 100-point mark with 36 goals and 68 assists in 2013–14.

Crosby has had a sensational run in his first ten seasons since being drafted, and much more is expected as he prepares for the second half of his career. All he needs to fulfill his promise is good health from this point forward.

#17

Bobby Clarke

Fifteen seasons with Philadelphia Flyers.

There's a certain level of awe that goes with nearly every player who ever won entry into the NHL's Hall of Fame. When the subject becomes the top fifty players in the sport's history, the genuflection is all but unanimous.

However, there are exceptions, and Bobby Clarke is one of those players who may not be praised with as much devotion by hockey purists as a Guy Lafleur, Bobby Hull, Wayne Gretzky, or Bobby Orr would be.

Career regular season:

1,144 games, 358 goals, 852 assists, 1,210 points

Three-time Hart Trophy winner (MVP)

One-time Bill Masterton Trophy winner (Perseverance and Sportsmanship)

One-time Frank Selke Trophy winner (Defensive Forward)

One-time Ted Lindsay Award winner (Most Outstanding Player)

Two-time first-team NHL All-Star; two-time second-team NHL All-Star

Two-time Stanley Cup champion

Advanced stats: 79.3 OPS, 26.8 DPS, 106.0 PS

Elected to Hall of Fame in 1987

There was a certain anger and viciousness that Clarke played with that inspired anger and resentment from many of his opponents and from non-Flyers fans around the league. Clarke always played with an edge and there is no doubt that he went over the line on several occasions when it came to helping his team win games.

Arguably nobody ever played with more effort and got every bit of talent out of his body than Clarke. And speaking of bodies, Clarke did not have the standard issue peak model that nearly all professional athletes have. Clarke was a diabetic, and he had to look after his condition every day if he wanted to play hockey.

There are a handful of professional athletes who have gone on to have long and productive careers even though they have had to confront their diabetes on an every-day basis, including Jay Cutler in football and Ron Santo in baseball, but Clarke was one of the first hockey players to do so. As a result, his draft status in 1969 was somewhat shaky.

He probably should have been the No. 1 choice that year, but teams were fearful of Clarke's condition and were afraid that he was not going to be able to have a long and productive career. Nobody made a move until the Philadelphia Flyers selected him in the second round with the No. 17 pick overall.

Bobby Clarke

Several NHL general managers regretted their hesitancy almost immediately after the Flyers made their selection. Sam Pollock of the Montreal Canadiens tried to induce a trade that would have put Clarke in a Habs uniform by offering a package of veteran players, but the Flyers refused to part with their draft choice. The Detroit Red Wings also came calling, but the Flyers were not budging.

As a rookie, Clarke was able to play in every game for the Flyers, and that clearly showed the rest of the league that he could manage his medical condition and play competitively. However, he did little to set himself apart from the rest of the competition with 15 goals and 31 assists. The Flyers finished fifth in the West Division and did not make the playoffs.

That season marked the last time anyone would describe Clarke as ordinary. In the 1970–71 season, Clarke's second in the league, he scored 27 goals and 36 assists for the Flyers and the team started to show a certain resiliency. While they lost to the Chicago Blackhawks in four games in the playoffs, the Flyers were creating a team built on tough play. Clarke often set the example for his teammates, and they began to follow him with furious devotion.

Clarke continued to improve in 1971–72, as he scored 35 goals and 46 assists and won the Bill Masterton Trophy that goes to the player who shows the most devotion to the game. By that season, Clarke's ability to maintain his medical routine became well-known around the sport, and that's why he was rewarded with the Masterson award for his perseverance.

The Flyers had a heartbreaking finish that year and did not make the playoffs, but that would not happen through the rest of Clarke's career. In fact, if Clarke had played with a tough and hard-nosed style up until that point, he clearly turned it up a couple of notches the following season.

Clarke scored 37 goals and 67 assists in 1972–73, and his 104 points was second in the league to Phil Esposito. However, when it came time to issue the Hart Trophy that goes to the league's Most Valuable Player, Clarke won the award even though Esposito had outscored him by 26 points and Orr had put another magical season on the board with 101 points.

While he played the game with arrogance and toughness on the ice, he was anything but that off the ice. When he learned that he had won the Hart Trophy, he was incredulous. "Are you kidding?" Clarke asked reporters. "If this award goes to the best player, it would go to Bobby Orr every year, hands down."

Clarke and the Flyers finished third in the West Division, and they defeated the Minnesota North Stars in six games in the playoffs to move to the semifinals. The Montreal Canadiens stopped them in five games, but their physical style became their signature. From that point forward, every Flyers opponent knew that a date with Clarke and the Flyers was going to be a major test.

The Flyers were fully formed by the 1973–74 season. There was a certain level of mayhem to their game, but the Broad Street Bullies were also extremely talented. They won the West Division with 112 points, as they beat out the Chicago Blackhawks for the top spot. They finished just one point behind the Boston Bruins for first place overall in the league.

Still, few thought the Flyers could beat elite teams like the New York Rangers or the Bruins in a best-of-seven playoff series. However, there was no lack of confidence in the Philadelphia locker room.

After the Flyers swept the Atlanta Flames in the opening round of the playoffs, they had to take on Jean Ratelle, Rod Gilbert, Brad Park, and goalie Ed Giacomin of the New York Rangers. The two teams battled on even terms for six games, but the Flyers asserted themselves in Game 7 at the Spectrum in Philadelphia and became the first expansion team to beat an Original Six team in the postseason.

It only got tougher in the Stanley Cup Final against Orr, Esposito, and the Big, Bad Bruins. Orr scored the game-winner late in Game 1, and it appeared the Bruins would take a 2-0 advantage as they led by a goal with less than a minute to go in Game 2. However, Philadelphia defenseman Moose Dupont tied the game with goalie Bernie Parent pulled, and the two teams went to overtime.

Bobby Clarke

Clarke jumped on a rebound in the extra session and shoveled the puck into the net for the series-tying goal. The Flyers had earned the victory they knew they had to have to win the series—and in Boston, nevertheless!—and while they were pressed hard by the Bruins in Game 6 in Philadelphia, the Flyers ultimately went on to win their first Stanley Cup.

They won their second straight title the next season, and once again Clarke played the role of the Flyers' leader. He won the second of his three Hart Trophies, and the Flyers stopped the Buffalo Sabres in six games in the Stanley Cup Final.

While the Flyers were a powerful and impressive team, they were widely resented around the NHL for their ruthless style of play. The NHL powerbrokers wanted to see a team that didn't rely on aggression and vicious play to intimidate opponents.

They got their wish, as the Montreal Canadiens unseated the Flyers in 1975–76, whipping them in four games in that season's Stanley Cup Final.

While Clarke and the Flyers would not be able to earn another Stanley Cup title throughout the rest of his 15-year career, he put his signature on the Flyers and the NHL and became one of the key figures in the history of the sport.

#18

Larry Robinson

Seventeen seasons with Montreal Canadiens. Three seasons with Los Angeles Kings.

It's not going too far to say that Larry Robinson was the best defenseman on the greatest team of all-time.

He also ranks with Montreal Canadiens legend Doug Harvey as perhaps the greatest defenseman in the history of the franchise. Robinson was certainly bigger, stronger and faster than Harvey, and his ability to take over a game and lock it down with vise-like strength helped the Canadiens win six Stanley Cups during his seventeen years with the *bleu, blanc, et rouge*.

Larry Robinson

Robinson played most of his career with two other superb defensemen on the Canadiens in Guy Lapointe and Serge Savard. All three could have been the No. 1 defenseman on 95 percent of the other teams in the NHL, but having "The Big Three" gave the Canadiens and head coach Scotty Bowman an advantage that would come into play in nearly every close game the Canadiens played.

Career regular season:
1,384 games, 208 goals, 750 assists, 958 points
Six Stanley Cup championships
Two-time James Norris Trophy winner (Best Defenseman)
One-time Conn Smythe Trophy winner (Playoff MVP)
Three-time first-team NHL All-Star
Three-time second-team NHL All-Star
Advanced stats: 60.5 OPS, 109.4 DPS, 170.0 PS
Elected to Hall of Fame in 1995

But as much as Lapointe and Savard contributed, Robinson was simply at another level. While he was more than competent when the Canadiens went on the attack, he was a huge wall of muscle in the defensive zone. Robinson was a 6-4, 225-pound aggressive and intelligent defenseman who broke up plays, pounded opponents mercilessly with his relentless physical style, and took the puck from them with ease.

He would regularly go on the attack after breaking up an opponent's rush, and while he was not Bobby Orr, Paul Coffey, or Nick Lidstrom, he wasn't far behind.

Robinson scored 10 or more goals in nine consecutive seasons for the Canadiens beginning in 1974–75, and he could have been a blueliner who scored 20 or more goals if that had been his priority.

Robinson could take over a game at any time. He did that in Game 5 of the 1978 Stanley Cup Finals against the Boston Bruins. The Bruins had just won two consecutive games to square the series at 2-2, and they had designs on continuing their momentum when the series returned to the Montreal Forum for Game 5.

Robinson refused to let that happen. The Habs went on a power play shortly after the midway point of the first period. The Bruins had given up just one shot to that point and the game was scoreless. Robinson took a short pass from Savard in the Montreal zone and took off down the right side. By the time he got to center ice he was at full speed. He engaged Bruins defenseman Mike Milbury, and Robinson raced by him and cut in towards the goal. Robinson moved the puck from his backhand to his forehand, took the measure of goalie Gerry Cheevers, and flipped the puck over his left shoulder for the opening goal of the game.

The Canadiens would go on to cruise to a 4-1 victory, and that Robinson goal appeared to demoralize the overmatched Bruins.

While that spectacular goal was one of Robinson's top individual highlights, he made game-changing plays on a regular basis.

Robinson had been drafted by the Canadiens in 1971—the same year they drafted Guy Lafleur—and Robinson was initially a bit reticent because the Habs had so many top-level defensemen and he feared that he might be stuck in the minor league for years. Yet his attitude quickly changed.

"It was the best thing that ever happened for my career," Robinson said. "I was with an organization that demanded quality, and backed it up with excellent coaches and instructors. I realized it was on me to improve every day and I got the support I needed to do just that."

As a rookie in 1972–73, Robinson got to play 36 games for a team that would eventually win the Stanley Cup. By the time the Canadiens returned to the Finals in 1976 against the hard-nosed Philadelphia Flyers, Robinson was an established star.

While the Flyers were the two-time defending Stanley Cup champions, many around the league were hoping the Canadiens could beat them because they did not like the mayhem associated with the Flyers. This was easier said than done, because the Flyers intimidated most of their opponents.

Robinson would not let this happen to the Canadiens. He bounced Flyer players nearly every time they came in the Montreal zone and he served as the Habs' policeman. He was the equalizer against players like Dave Schultz, Bob Kelly, and Don Saleski, and his no-nonsense attitude allowed the Canadiens' skill to take over and sweep the series.

Playing that kind of role did not come naturally for Robinson. "It took a lot to get me upset, especially in my early years," Robinson explained. "But once I started to play with a bit of a temper and a physical edge, that gave me more freedom. When I was able to hit somebody or deliver a hard check early, I found that I had more skating room later in the game."

Robinson was regularly at his best in the playoffs, and he was never better than he was in 1978, when the Canadiens won their third straight title and he won the Conn Smythe Trophy. In addition to his pivotal goal against the Bruins, he tied Lafleur with a postseason-high 21 points, and that included a league-best 17 assists. He had two goals and four assists in the Stanley Cup Final series.

The Canadiens reeled off four straight titles from 1976 through 1979, and those Montreal teams may have been the best that ever played the game. Robinson remembers those teams as the great joy of his career. "We might have lost eight games one year, 10 games the next, and maybe 12 the year after," Robinson said. "Everyone on the team was committed to winning, and there were no letdowns. We played hard every night and there was nothing more rewarding than playing with teammates who were that good and that committed to winning."

While the Stanley Cups that the Canadiens won in the late 1970s were a perfect example of a dominant team playing at its peak, the 1986 Stanley Cup was a surprise. That year the Canadiens finished with a pedestrian 40-33-7 record and little was expected with rookie goalie Patrick Roy in the net. However, they defeated Boston, Hartford, and the New York Rangers in the first three rounds of the playoffs before dispatching the Calgary Flames in five games.

That was the last of the titles that Robinson would earn in his career. He would eventually sign a free-agent contract with the Los

Angeles Kings, and he would play three more years on the West Coast until he retired after the 1991–92 season.

Robinson's team made the playoffs in each of his twenty years in the NHL, giving him a unique legacy and an utterly brilliant career.

#19

Ken Dryden

Eight seasons with Montreal Canadiens.

Every once in a while, a team will bring up a minor leaguer from its farm system towards the end of the regular season with the hope that the player will have the energy and talent to give his squad a lift in the playoffs.

Sometimes that kind of shot in the dark works, but most times it doesn't. However, there has never been an instance where a call-up has had the sensational impact that Ken Dryden had when the Montreal Canadiens recalled him late in the 1970–71 season.

Career regular season:
397 games, 258-57-74, 2.24 goals-against average, 46 shutouts
Five-time Vezina Trophy winner (Top Goaltender)
Five-time first-team NHL All-Star; one-time second-team NHL All-Star
Six-time Stanley Cup winner
Elected to Hall of Fame in 1983

Dryden was an unusual goalie because he was big and gangly at 6-foot-4 and he was quite awkward-looking with his short leg pads on his outsized frame.

The Canadiens were hoping that Dryden might be able to give starting goalie Rogie Vachon some relief before the playoffs, and many observers were skeptical. They thought Dryden would not have the reactions at his size to compete with the quick skaters and hard shooters he would confront in the NHL.

Even if Dryden could play decently in a few regular-season games, there was no way that Montreal head coach Al MacNeil would consider using him in the playoffs, or so the Canadiens' media core thought.

Dryden, a former All-American from Cornell, aced his regular-season exam. He earned a 6-0-0 record in his late-season work with an eye-popping 1.65 goals-against average.

MacNeil decided to take a chance on letting Dryden play in the postseason. This was not one of Montreal's better regular-season teams, as they finished third in the East Division, 24 points behind the explosive and powerful Boston Bruins.

The Bruins were the defending Stanley Cup champions, and the 1970–71 season was magical for them. The Bruins had a marauding team of high-scoring and talented players, and they were led by Bobby Orr and Phil Esposito. By this time, Orr was at his peak while Esposito set the NHL record with 76 goals and 152 points.

The Canadiens had tormented the Bruins for years in the postseason, but this appeared to be a runaway for the Bruins—at least on paper. Surely, they would finally get a chance to take out their frustration on the Habs.

Ken Dryden

And when the Bruins fans saw Dryden in the net, they could barely contain themselves. They thought they would be able to score on the rookie at will. Boston Garden fans jeered at Dryden, and shouted that "the Bruins ain't Hah-vud, kid."

The Bruins won the first game by a 3-1 score and it was rather routine. However, they had the Canadiens on the ropes in Game 2 when they jumped to a 5-1 second period lead. It wasn't a question of whether the Bruins would win; the issue was whether they would reach double figures against Dryden.

But the Canadiens were true professionals, and they just kept on working. Henri Richard scored a late second-period goal and Jean Beliveau scored two early in the third period. Suddenly, the rout had turned into a close game and the Habs had the momentum. They continued to press the action and Dryden stopped everything that came his way. Montreal earned a 7-5 comeback win that sent shock-waves throughout the NHL.

The series shifted back to Montreal and the two teams split at the Forum. The Bruins appeared to regain control with a 7-3 win in the pivotal fifth game, but the Habs smacked the Big Bad Bruins in Montreal 8-3 to tie the series in Game 6.

The Bruins expected to dominate in Game 7, and they came out with a powerful offensive effort. However, Dryden was calm, cool, and collected. He kicked out shot after shot, and Esposito slammed his stick on the ice in frustration and labeled Dryden "a thieving giraffe." Montreal won the game 4-2, and Dryden was the hero.

The Habs went on to beat the Minnesota North Stars in six games and they met the high-scoring Chicago Blackhawks in the Final. With Bobby Hull and Stan Mikita at the top of their game, Chicago was expected to come away with the Stanley Cup. However, the big rookie goalie wouldn't let that happen and the Habs won the title by beating the Blackhawks in seven games. Once again, Dryden led his team to the series win with a stellar performance on the road.

Dryden was named the Conn Smythe Trophy winner and because he had only played six games during the previous season, he was still considered a rookie in 1971–72. He earned the Calder Trophy as the NHL's rookie of the year as well.

After that brilliant start to his career, Dryden soon established himself as one of the top goalies in the league, and by the end of his eight-year run in Montreal, he had taken it even further.

Dryden was one of the best goalies to ever play in the league. His team won the Stanley Cup in six of his eight years, and while he retired at the end of the 1978–79 season, he had established that he was always at his best when the Canadiens were playing the most important games.

It didn't hurt that the Canadiens were most likely the top team the game has ever seen between 1976 and 1979, but much of that was due to Dryden's excellence in net.

Opponents knew they had to be at their absolute best to try to skate on even terms with the Canadiens in any game, and even if they managed that, they had to contend with perhaps the best goalie in the history of the game.

Dryden's career was relatively short, especially when you measure it against the other greats in the game and at his position. However, he won the Vezina Trophy five times and was in goal for six Montreal Stanley Cups. That's a measure of excellence and execution that no other goalie can match.

#20

Nicklas Lidstrom

Twenty seasons with Detroit Red Wings.

Given the scintillating level at which Nicklas Lidstrom performed throughout the entirety of his brilliant twenty-year career with the Detroit Red Wings, it's shocking to note that he was a third-round draft choice who was the No. 53 overall pick in 1989.

When it was all said and done, Lidstrom was one of the most dynamic players to compete in his era, and even though he had remarkable physical gifts like skating speed, velocity when shooting the puck, and picture-perfect accuracy when passing, it was

Career regular season:
1,564 games, 264 goals, 878 assists, 1,142 points
One-time Conn Smythe Trophy winner (Playoff MVP)
Seven-time Norris Trophy winner (Best Defenseman)
Eleven-time first-team NHL All-Star; two-time second-team NHL All-Star
Advanced stats: 98.1 OPS, 113.6 DPS, 211.8 PS
Four-time Stanley Cup champion
Elected to Hall of Fame in 2015

the way he saw the game develop that set him apart from the competition.

Hockey at the NHL level was chess to a grand master on the level of Bobby Fischer or Boris Spassky. He saw a play develop before most—usually three moves ahead of everybody else.

Lidstrom met every challenge, and it didn't take long for him to prove himself. He was a dynamic force in his rookie year with the Red Wings as he scored 11 goals and 49 assists and finished second in the rookie of the year voting to Vancouver speedster and Russian import Pavel Bure.

Lidstrom used that rookie season as a jumping-off point. He didn't demonstrate many weaknesses early on, but in his first few years he learned the tendencies of his teammates and his opponents. By the time he got to his fifth and sixth seasons in the league, he knew all the nuances of how the game would unfold. His intelligence made him such a dangerous player.

Mike Babcock coached Lidstrom for the last eight years of his career, and on his way to Lidstrom's retirement announcement at the end of the 2011–12 season, he called former Red Wings coach Scotty Bowman to discuss the player who had been such a key part of so many important Red Wings victories over the years.

"When I talked to Scotty, the word he used when discussing Nicklas was 'perfect,' and I agree with that assessment," Babcock said. "What he meant to the organization was incredible. He was just a brilliant player, and he was a better human being than he was an athlete."

Nicklas Lidstrom

Lidstrom never came to the locker room prepared to give anything but his best effort, whether it was the first game of the season in October, or the last game of the Stanley Cup Final in June. That ability helped the Red Wings make the playoffs every year of his career, and they got to hoist the Stanley Cup four times.

Lidstrom was an offensive dynamo when he gained possession of the puck. He scored a career-high 20 goals in 1999–2000 and also had 53 assists as he made the NHL's first All-Star team for the third straight year, and he finished second in the Norris Trophy voting.

He won the NHL's best defenseman honors in 2001–02 for the first time. By the end of his career, he had won the honor seven times. Only Bobby Orr (eight) won the honor more often than Lidstrom.

Teammate Chris Chelios, who earned Hall of Fame status himself in 2013 and won the Norris Trophy three times, called Lidstrom the best defenseman who had ever played the game.

"I played with Larry Robinson. I played against [Raymond] Bourque. You go even further with Doug Harvey," Chelios said. "But in my opinion there couldn't have been anyone better than Nicklas Lidstrom."

While one can question whether Lidstrom was as spectacular or as impactful as Orr, he certainly had the benefit of good health that evaded the Bruins' defenseman.

Lidstrom was able to compete at the very highest level until his retirement. Consistency was his hallmark, and while he did not make flashy plays very often, he always made the right play.

"What makes Nick great is he's very good to great at everything. He doesn't have any wow factor," said Detroit general manager Ken Holland. "The wow factor is, he does it every day, day after day after day, after game, after year. Big games, small games. The wow factor is the constant that you just know. It's the body of work."

If there was a "wow" factor for Lidstrom, it was his play on defense. His ability to diagnose a play before it developed allowed him to use his skating speed to get to a spot to break up a play, or put his stick in a position to steal or deflect the puck out of trouble. He could play the physical game when he needed to, but nobody was close to him when it came to outplaying, outthinking, or outworking his opponents.

Red Wings broadcast analyst Larry Murphy has one of the most unique perspectives on Lidstrom. He partnered with him on the blue line for the last few years of his Hall of Fame career before he moved to the TV booth after his retirement.

"His biggest strength is his positioning and not overexerting himself," said Murphy. "He's very effective from the start to the finish of the game because he never takes an unnecessary step. He's always in the right position. His timing is always impeccable. He's not going to assert himself offensively unless it's a glaring opportunity or the team is behind. He just conserves energy. Because he's so efficient out there, the game comes easy to him."

Lidstrom's tendencies towards perfection did not just manifest itself in games. He showed his desire to play the game the right way in practice. Babcock said it was 50 to 60 games during his first season as head coach of the Red Wings before he saw Lidstrom make a simple mistake. During a practice session, Lidstrom made a poor pass in a breakout drill.

Lidstrom was remarkably productive on the offensive end throughout his career. He scored 10 or more goals in fourteen of fifteen seasons between 1993–94 and 2008–09, and the only year he failed to reach that level he scored nine goals. His passing was pinpoint, and he averaged 43.9 assists per season.

Consider Orr one of Lidstrom's biggest supporters. Orr is far too modest to ever compare other great players to himself in terms of ranking, but he was a big fan of the way Lidstrom got it done on the ice.

"He sure put up the numbers," Orr told hockey writer Pierre LeBrun. "He does it differently than the way I did with the end-to-end play. I've seen replays of his shots from the point—he gets them through, always on the net. He's not trying to put it through the end boards."

Nicklas Lidstrom

When Lidstrom retired at the age of forty-two, it was not because he'd lost his effectiveness. However, Lidstrom felt he couldn't prepare for the games as thoroughly as he once did or bring it every single day, so he called it a career.

Babcock lamented the decision, because he knew that Lidstrom would be missed in the lockerroom as much as he would be missed for his on-ice contributions.

"You never had any trouble with Nick as the coach because he was always prepared and motivated," Babcock said. "Nick brings it every single day, sets an example for all of us in professionalism and perfection and work ethic and doing it without ego."

He was a truly remarkable player and remains a remarkable individual.

#21

Frank Mahovlich

Twelve seasons with Toronto Maple Leafs. Four seasons with Detroit Red Wings. Four seasons with Montreal Canadiens. Four seasons with the World Hockey Association (Toronto Toros and Birmingham Bulls).

Big, fast, powerful, and gifted, Frank Mahovlich had the look of a hockey superstar long before he ever had a chance to skate in the NHL.

He was touted as an elite player every step of his development, and there was little doubt that he would become an impact player once he slipped on an NHL uniform. That came in the 1957-58 season as a rookie with the Toronto Maple Leafs.

Frank Mahovlich

Mahovlich was playing for the team in his own backyard, and the heat was on from the beginning. He won the Calder Trophy as the league's rookie of the year as a nineteen-year-old, beating out Chicago's Bobby Hull as he scored 20 goals and 36 assists. But while there was flash, production, and execution, there wasn't much joy for Mahovlich.

He was filled with nervous tension, and when he

Career regular season:
NHL: 1,181 games, 533 goals, 570 assists, 1,103 points. WHA: 237 games, 89 goals, 143 assists, 232 points
One-time Calder Trophy winner (Rookie of the Year)
Three-time first-team NHL All-Star; six-time second-team NHL All-Star
Six-time Stanley Cup winner
Elected to Hall of Fame in 1981
Advanced stats: 99.4 OPS, 22.3 DPS, 121.7 PS

didn't have great games, it ate him up inside. When he did, he worried if he would produce the next games. Worse than the anxiety was his silence about it. He couldn't let anybody know how nervous he was or how terrible he felt, and that would eventually take its toll years later. This was the late 1950s, and men did not talk about their feelings. Particularly men who were professional athletes.

It might have been all right if Mahovlich had a perceptive coach who realized that his productive young player was quite troubled. Instead, it was just the opposite. Punch Imlach was a demanding, hard-bitten coach who wanted his players to produce.

He pushed hard and he didn't give any breaks—particularly to Mahovlich, who was gifted (cursed) by so much natural ability.

If Mahovlich scored a goal, Imlach wanted two. If he scored two, Imlach wanted a hat trick and better passing. Nothing was good enough for the coach, and he would not hesitate to lecture and ridicule Mahovlich regularly.

That didn't stop "The Big M" from producing or the Leafs from winning. During the 1960-61 season, Mahovlich started putting the puck in the net at a level that scouts had anticipated when the Leafs first inserted him into the lineup. His slapshot was deadly accurate and his timing was impeccable. He got off to a powerful start, and he had registered 48 goals with 14 games remaining in the season.

He would break the NHL single-season record if he could score three goals during the remaining games and get to 51.

The goals never came, as Mahovlich went into an end-of-season freeze and he finished with 48, and that was second to Montreal's Bernie Geoffrion, who hit the 50 mark.

Mahovlich was the NHL's first-team All-Star left winger, and that began a streak of six straight seasons in which he was either a first- or second-team All-Star. However, he did not come close to the 40-goal mark in any of those seasons and there was always something a tad underwhelming about Mahovlich's production.

While Mahovlich didn't put the puck in the net for the Leafs the way he had in the 1960-61 season, the Leafs reeled off three straight championships between 1962 and '64. If Mahovlich's regular-season scoring was a bit of a head scratcher, his playoff production was exactly what the Leafs expected from him.

He scored six goals and six assists during the Leafs' 12-game championship run in 1962, and he put four goals and 11 assists on the board during their 14-game run in 1964.

Three straight championships did not ease Mahovlich's burden. Imlach regularly gave his star a hard time, and fans booed him regularly at Toronto home games. Mahovlich's tension and anxiety increased as he bottled up his feelings and never acknowledged them.

That pressure was having an impact, and he had what was referred to as a "nervous breakdown" early in the 1967-68 season. He was hospitalized in Toronto and missed 11 games. Eventually he returned and the fans welcomed him with concern, but it was clear that he needed to get out of Toronto.

The Maple Leafs traded him to the Detroit Red Wings that season, and that lifted a great weight from his shoulders. Mahovlich started to play free-and-easy hockey with the Red Wings, and since

Frank Mahovlich

Gordie Howe was the king in that city, the Big M's previous burdens never returned. Mahovlich scored 49 goals in 1968-69, and he established himself as one of the league's best players once again.

Players who knew Mahovlich in Toronto couldn't believe the change in his personality. Instead of feeling the immense pressure that nearly destroyed him, he played with joy as he had a chance to play with Howe and Alex Delvecchio. Another big bonus was the presence of his younger brother Peter Mahovlich, known as "The Little M." Peter Mahovlich may have been the younger brother, but he had five inches on his older sibling.

The Red Wings were struggling in the 1970-71 season, and they traded the elder Mahovlich to the Montreal Canadiens that year. While Montreal was a solid and veteran team with a history of brilliance in the playoffs, nobody expected them to survive a playoff confrontation with the explosive Boston Bruins.

However, Mahovlich played a key role as the Canadiens were not intimidated by the Big, Bad Bruins, and they eliminated them in seven games. The Canadiens went on to beat the Minnesota North Stars and Chicago Blackhawks en route to a Stanley Cup. Mahovlich was magnificent during the championship run, as he netted 14 goals and added 13 assists for the Habs.

While the spotlight was probably even greater in Montreal than it was in Toronto, Mahovlich thrived throughout his tenure with the Canadiens. He scored 43 goals in his first full season there, and followed up with 38 and 31 goals, respectively.

Mahovlich could have stayed with the Canadiens and become a franchise fixture, but he had a chance to move on in his career and sign a big-money contract with the World Hockey Association. Although he was originally the property of that league's Houston Aeros, he was traded to the Toronto Toros. This time, the pressure of playing in Toronto did not bother The Big M and he put back-to-back seasons of 38 and 34 goals together.

The Toros struggled to gain acceptance while competing in the same city as the Maple Leafs, and they pulled up stakes and moved to Birmingham, Alabama. Mahovlich went with them and tried to establish hockey in the Deep South, but that part of the country was not yet ready for hockey.

Mahovlich called it a career at that point, and his numbers made him a sure-fire Hall of Famer.

#22

Paul Coffey

Twelve seasons with Edmonton Oilers. Five seasons with Pittsburgh Penguins. Four seasons with Detroit Red Wings. Three years with Hartford Whalers/Carolina Hurricanes. Two years with Los Angeles Kings. Two years with Philadelphia Flyers. One year with Boston Bruins.

From the very beginning, Paul Coffey had the skating ability to be taken seriously as a candidate to play in the NHL. From the time he started playing as a small four- and five-year-old, he always skated better than the other kids in his age group.

Career regular season:

NHL: 1,409 games, 396 goals, 1,135 assists, 1,531 points.

WHA: 52 games, 1 goal, 10 assists

Three-time Norris Trophy winner (Best Defenseman)

Four-time first-team NHL All-Star; four-time second-team NHL All-Star

Four-time Stanley Cup winner

Elected to Hall of Fame in 2004

Advanced stats: 117.0 OPS, 68.7 DPS, 185.7 PS

Coffey had the ability to skate with speed, skate with power, and skate with agility. It was a gift, but not one he took for granted. He took skating classes to improve his balance and power, because he knew that "good enough" simply was not good enough. He had to get better if he was going to achieve his goal and play in the NHL.

Coffey had heard from scouts and coaches that he had the tools to keep climbing the ladder, and by the time he was eligible for the 1980 draft, there were indications that he would go early. The Edmonton Oilers made good on those rumors and selected him with the sixth pick of the first round.

The Oilers kept him at the major league level in 1980–81, and while he did not put up the prolific scoring numbers right away that he would shortly thereafter, he felt comfortable playing in the NHL as a nineteen-year-old. He scored nine goals and 23 assists as a rookie and he showed a willingness to mix it up with older and bigger players as he collected 130 penalty minutes.

Coffey was known for his scoring and skating throughout his career, but he was never afraid to engage other players in an effort to stand up for himself and his teammates. It was not that Coffey was a notable tough guy—he wasn't—but he certainly wasn't going to back down. That willingness to show that he could handle himself was instrumental in him becoming a top offensive defenseman because it would buy him some extra space when skating with the puck and creating.

Paul Coffey

Coffey also received plenty of encouragement from his partners on defense. In his early years, veteran Lee Fogolin showed him the ropes while Garry Lariviere gave him some freedom on the ice.

Lariviere knew what kind of skater Coffey was, and he figured that if he could help Coffey play his offensive game, he would be helping the Oilers.

"I hear you've got the wheels," Lariviere said. "Any time you want to go, go. I'll be back here for you."

That was all Coffey needed to hear. He started venturing up the ice and often played as a fourth forward in the offensive zone.

At the time Coffey was establishing himself as a top offensive defenseman in the NHL, the Oilers were establishing themselves as the next up-and-coming team in the league. During his early years, the New York Islanders were in the midst of a championship run, but the Oilers got their turn in 1983–84.

That was Coffey's fourth season in the league. By that time he had established himself as one of the Oilers' most explosive scorers and he was clearly one of the top offensive defensemen in the league. He had scored 29 goals in his second and his third years, but he really came on with a rush in 83-84 with a remarkable 40-goal, 86-assist season.

Those numbers were reminiscent of what Bobby Orr had done in his glory years with the Boston Bruins, and the Oilers were the same kind of offensive juggernaut that the Bruins had been in the early 1970s. The only difference was that the Oilers were more efficient and more disciplined, and they accomplished more.

Instead of winning two Stanley Cups in three seasons like the Bruins, the Oilers won three Stanley Cups in four years during Coffey's tenure in Edmonton.

Coffey asserted himself in dominant fashion as the Oilers won their first Stanley Cup in 1984. He scored eight goals and 14 assists in that run, and he was a remarkable plus-21 as the Oilers completed their rise to the top with a five-game victory over the four-time champion Islanders.

If Coffey was good that year, he was even better the next with 12 goals and 25 assists from his spot on the blue line. He scored four game-winning goals in the postseason and connected on a remarkable 18.2 percent of his shots.

The Oilers put on a ridiculous offensive display that year as they scored 98 goals in 18 playoff games. The Oilers took home their second straight Stanley Cup as they beat the Philadelphia Flyers in five games, but it was in the Western Conference Final against the Chicago Blackhawks that they did their most formidable scoring.

They scored 44 goals in their six-game victory, including 11 goals in the first game in the series and 10 in the fifth. Both of those wins came at home, but they clinched the series with an 8-2 victory in Chicago.

The 1985–86 season represented the peak of Coffey's offensive fireworks. He scored 48 goals and 90 assists, and that represented the second-highest scoring season for any defenseman. He finished one point behind Bobby Orr, who had scored a record 139 points during the Bruins 1970–71 season.

The Oilers were a team with remarkable talent, and they were led by the redoubtable Wayne Gretzky and the relentless Mark Messier. On another team, Coffey would have been the star of stars, but on the Oilers, he was one more great player.

"It was a team of destiny," explained Coffey. "Any time you not only have the best player in the game but he's the hardest worker on your team, then add Messier, Anderson, Kurri, myself, Kevin Lowe, as well as every other player on those hockey teams, you've got a very, very talented group, and if you're a hardworking team—and we were—good things can happen. It was a lot of fun. It was a great hockey club, we enjoyed playing, we enjoyed each other's company, and when you have those things, a lot of good things can happen, and for us, it was championships."

As explosive as Coffey was, he was traded during the 1987–88 season to the Pittsburgh Penguins. After winning three Stanley Cups with the Oilers, he added another with the Penguins. He also got to play with Mario Lemieux in his prime, and Coffey was thrilled to play with the gifted superstar.

Coffey moved around quite a bit in the final years of his career, but he established himself as one of the most explosive defensemen in NHL history and a four-time Stanley Cup champion.

#23

Bryan Trottier

Fifteen seasons with New York Islanders. Three seasons with Pittsburgh Penguins.

Mike Bossy was the sniper, Denis Potvin was the All–Star defenseman, and Billy Smith was the battling goaltender who stopped nearly every shot that came his way.

However, if you had to name one indispensable player from the New York Islanders dynasty that won four straight Stanley Cups from 1980 through 1983, it would have to be Bryan Trottier.

Bryan Trottier

Younger fans who did not get a chance to see Trottier play missed out on one of the best all-around players the game has ever seen. Think of Jonathan Toews of the Chicago Blackhawks and Patrice Bergeron of the Boston Bruins. Meld the two of those players together and pick out the best attributes of both and you have the brilliant Trottier.

Trottier may not have the statistics to match up with Wayne Gretzky, Mario Lemieux, or Mark Messier, but he was unstoppable when it came to making plays that helped his team win in the Stanley Cup playoffs.

Career regular season:
1,279 games, 524 goals, 901 assists, 1,424 points
One-time Conn Smythe Trophy winner (Playoff MVP)
One-time Hart Trophy winner (MVP)
One-time Art Ross Trophy winner (High Scorer)
One-time King Clancy Award winner (Leadership and Humanitarian Contribution)
One-time Calder Trophy winner (Rookie of the Year)
Two-time first-team NHL All-Star; two-time second-team All-Star
Six-time Stanley Cup champion
Advanced stats: 94.1 OPS, 26.1 DPS, 120.2 PS
Elected to Hall of Fame in 1997

Nobody saw Trottier as that kind of player when he was drafted in the second round of the 1974 amateur draft. Trottier was the 22nd player selected overall, and he was seen as a solid player who would one day be able to contribute at the NHL level.

The Islanders saw him as more than that when they drafted him at the age of seventeen. However, they also saw that he was in need of further development, and they asked him to spend one more year at the junior level with Lethbridge of the West Coast Junior Hockey League.

The move paid dividends as Trottier scored 46 goals and 98 assists in his final year of junior hockey, and he was ready to play at the NHL level at the start of the 1975–76 season.

Trottier made a seamless transition to the NHL, scoring 32 goals and 63 assists in his rookie year and running away with the Calder Trophy over teammate Glenn "Chico" Resch, Dennis "Pee-Wee" Maruk of the California Golden Seals, and Mel Bridgman of the Philadelphia Flyers.

The Islanders had him centering rugged left wing Clark Gillies and sharp-shooting Billy Harris, and he started to establish himself in the second game of the season when he scored three goals and two assists.

But Trottier was not just an offensive star. He showed remarkable defensive tenacity from the start, and head coach Al Arbour did not hesitate to put him on the ice against the opponents' best offensive players. Trottier may not have been as savvy as some of the top veteran defensive players, but he was technically sound and never made the same mistake twice.

Eventually, Mike Bossy would replace Harris on the top line, and the Trottier-Bossy-Gillies combination would become the most dominant and consistent in the league.

By the late 1970s, the Islanders were emerging as an up-and-coming power in the NHL. While they would not win the Stanley Cup, Arbour's team was getting better every year and it seemed it was just a matter of time before the Islanders would take the baton from the Montreal Canadiens and Guy Lafleur, who would win four titles in a row between 1976 and 1979.

Trottier was at the peak of his offensive game from 1977 to 1979. He was a first-team All-Star in both seasons, and he scored 46 goals and 77 assists and was second in the Hart Trophy race in '77-78.

There was no settling for second place the following year. He was relentless from the start of the year and he scored 47 goals and 87 assists for a league-best 134 points. He came away with the Hart Trophy, besting Lafleur, Marcel Dionne of the Los Angeles Kings, and Potvin.

The Islanders were poised to take the title that season from the Canadiens. They finished with a league-best 116 points, one more than Montreal. If the two teams had met in the playoffs, the Islanders would have had home-ice advantage.

However, the Islanders were shocked by the cross-town New York Rangers. Phil Esposito and goalie John Davidson led the Rangers to a six-game upset of the Islanders.

That loss may have hurt, but it served a purpose. It steeled the Islanders for what it would take to win the Stanley Cup. No matter how talented a team was, it could not let up at any point. Trottier was the one who drove this point home to his teammates.

The Islanders did not have a great regular season in 1979–80, as they finished second in the Patrick Division to the record-setting Philadelphia Flyers. Not only did the Flyers outdistance the Islanders by 25 points (116-91), but also Philadelphia set the NHL and North American pro sports record by going undefeated in 35 straight games.

But the Islanders knew that regular-season achievements meant little, and they came out in the playoffs prepared and ready to win. They took out the Kings and the Bruins in the first two rounds, losing just two games in the two series, before meeting the high-scoring Buffalo Sabres in the semifinals. The Islanders whipped the Sabres in six games.

Every time the Islanders needed an important goal, it seemed like Trottier scored it or set it up with the pass. He scored 12 goals and 17 assists in that playoff season.

When the Islanders went to the Final, it was against their rivals from Philadelphia. While many were impressed by Philadelphia's regular-season achievements and all-around play, Trottier knew the Islanders were the better team.

"We had full confidence that we could win that series," Trottier said. "We had full respect for the Flyers, but we believed that if we played our best hockey, we would win."

The Islanders prevailed and won their first title when Bob Nystrom scored the series-clinching goal in overtime of the sixth game. The Nassau Coliseum fans went wild as their beloved team clinched the title at home and Trottier was named the postseason MVP.

Trottier was amazingly consistent in the playoffs, as he scored 29 points in each of the next two playoff seasons as well, and the Islanders won the title in both of those seasons against the Minnesota North Stars and Vancouver Canucks, respectively. They also won the following year, but Trottier was "held" to 20 points as the Islanders clinched the title against the Edmonton Oilers.

Gretzky and the Oilers stopped the Islanders the following year, and while the Islanders remained a strong team, they did not get back to the championship round.

Eventually, Trottier was signed as a free agent by the emerging Pittsburgh Penguins prior to the 1990–91 season, and Trottier helped them mature and win back-to-back Stanley Cups.

Trottier had a brilliant 18-year playing career in the NHL, and he was a star player on six Stanley Cup winning teams. Few players have ever been able to match his contributions as an all-around player.

#24

Jaromir Jagr
(through 2014–15)

Eleven seasons with Pittsburgh Penguins. Four seasons with New York Rangers. Three seasons with Washington Capitals. Two seasons with New Jersey Devils. One season with Philadelphia Flyers. One season with Dallas Stars. One season with Boston Bruins. One season with Florida Panthers.

Jaromir Jagr is the hockey player who simply would not go away.
In the beginning, Jagr was the wunderkind who brought his dramatic and game-breaking talent with him from Kladno,

Career regular season:

NHL: 1,550 games, 722 goals, 1,080 assists, 1,802 points.

Five-time Art Ross Trophy winner (Leading Scorer)

One-time Hart Trophy winner (MVP)

Three-time Ted Lindsay Award winner (Most Outstanding Player)

Seven-time first-team NHL All-Star; one-time second-team NHL All-Star

Two-time Stanley Cup winner

Advanced stats: 165.1 OPS, 37.1 DPS, 202.4 PS

Czechoslovakia. He was the No. 5 pick in the 1990 draft by the Pittsburgh Penguins, and he played with the Penguins as an eighteen-year-old rookie.

Blessed with size, strength, skating ability, and tremendous skill, Jagr did not have the responsibility of carrying his team to the playoffs and turning them into a contender. Jagr was playing with Mario Lemieux, who was at the top of his game and in a position to dominate. The Penguins looked like one of the best teams in the league without Jagr, but once he became part of the mix, the Pens were odds-on favorites to win the Stanley Cup.

Jagr fit right in on this talented team and he had an excellent rookie season with 27 goals and 30 assists. The Penguins lived up to expectations as they won the Patrick Division title and then dominated in the postseason.

The Penguins beat the New Jersey Devils and Washington Capitals in the first two rounds, but they met a solid Boston Bruins team that had earned 12 more points than the Penguins in the regular season. Boston won the first two games of the series, but the skill on the Penguins soon took over as Lemieux, Jagr, and Kevin Stevens dominated the rest of the way and the Pens took the series in six games.

Another tough series appeared to be at hand as the Penguins went after the franchise's first Stanley Cup against the Western Conference champion Minnesota North Stars. While Minnesota was tough and feisty and won two games in the series, the talent on the Penguins dominated and they won the series in six games.

The following year, Jagr continued to establish himself. He broke the 30-goal mark for the first time in his career, and he scored 30 or more for the next twelve seasons. He also added 37 assists.

If he was good during the regular season, he was even better in the playoffs, as the Penguins rolled to their second straight Stanley Cup. After beating the Capitals, New York Rangers, and Bruins in the first three rounds of the playoffs, the Penguins had a matchup with the Chicago Blackhawks in the Stanley Cup Final.

The Blackhawks had caught fire in the playoffs, as they had beaten the St. Louis Blues, Detroit Red Wings, and Edmonton Oilers, and since they had passed all their playoff tests, many thought Chicago had the ability to push the Penguins to the limit and possibly take the series in seven games.

Jagr was not about to let that happen. He scored 11 goals and 13 assists in the postseason, and he had key goals in both the first and fourth games as the Penguins recorded a sweep in the series.

Jagr was 2-for-2 in Stanley Cup championships, and it looked like he might have a career like Jean Beliveau where he would rack up a slew of Stanley Cups throughout his career.

That has not happened. Jagr has not had a chance to hoist the Stanley Cup since his first two seasons, but he has become one of the most gifted and talented players in league history.

Remarkably, Jagr developed a knack for scoring clutch goals throughout his career. He was at his best in the 1995–96 season, as he scored 62 goals and 87 assists. Jagr scored 12 game-winning goals that year, and it seemed that Jagr was almost always involved if the Penguins needed a tying or go-ahead goal in the third period that season.

Jagr did not win the league's scoring championship that season, as that honor would go to Lemieux, who accumulated 161 points. Despite that brilliant 1-2 punch, the Penguins were beaten in the Eastern Conference Final by the upset-minded Florida Panthers in seven games.

Lemieux retired in 1997, and that's when Jagr finally got his chance to win the scoring title. He did that in 1997–98 with 102 points, and he also won the scoring title each of the next two years.

While the Penguins were no longer a serious threat to win the Stanley Cup after Lemieux retired, Jagr still was able to make a run at Olympic glory. He led the Czechs to the gold medal game at the 1998 Winter Olympics in Nagano, Japan, and the Czechs upset the Russians 1-0 in the title game.

Jagr was traded by the Penguins to the Washington Capitals prior to the 2001–02 season, and while he played well with the Caps for two-and-a-half seasons, he wasn't the dominant player that the Caps had hoped he would be.

They traded him to the Rangers shortly after the midway point of the 2003–04 season, and he found his stride with the Rangers in the 2005–06 season. Jagr scored 54 goals and 69 assists and finished as the league's second-leading scorer behind Joe Thornton. Despite Jagr's powerful season, the Rangers were beaten in the first round of the playoffs by the Devils, and they seemed far away from fighting for a championship.

Jagr was frustrated, and he left the Rangers and the NHL for three full seasons while he played in the KHL.

But while Jagr was gone, he was not forgotten. He came back to the league in 2011–12 and signed a free-agent contract with the Flyers. The following year, he signed with the Dallas Stars and he appeared to be someone who could help the team get back to the playoffs. However, when the Stars fell out of the playoff race near the trade deadline in the 2012–13 season, he was traded to the Boston Bruins.

The Bruins were looking for their second Stanley Cup in three seasons, and he would get closer to the championship than he had been since his first two seasons. The Bruins rallied to a near-miraculous win over the Toronto Maple Leafs in the first round before rolling over the Rangers and the Penguins.

They met the Blackhawks in the Stanley Cup Final, and the Bruins got close when they took a 2-1 series lead, but they lost the series in six games.

Jaromir Jagr (through 2014–15)

The following year, Jagr signed with the Devils, and by the end of the 2014–15 season he was taking a leadership role with the Florida Panthers at the age of forty-three.

Jagr says he wants to play until he's fifty. After scoring 17 goals and 30 assists in 2014–15, he may just be able to meet his goal.

#25

Marcel Dionne

Twelve seasons with Los Angeles Kings. Four seasons with Detroit Red Wings. Three seasons with New York Rangers.

It does not seem to make much sense. When Marcel Dionne was on the ice, he was one of the most spectacular players the game has ever seen. Few players could ever match him in speed or quickness, and those who could simply did not have offensive skills.

The presence of Dionne in any game was an eye-catching experience for fans and opponents. "Where's Dionne?" was the question that had to be asked at the start of any game, and as soon as he came on the

Marcel Dionne

ice, fans would rise to their feet so they would not miss any of his dazzling moves.

But here's the part that doesn't make sense. A good part of Dionne's hockey career was played in obscurity. He was one of the greatest junior players of his era, but he was not the No. 1 draft choice in 1971. That was the same year that Guy Lafleur became eligible for the NHL draft. Lafleur, of course, was selected first by the Montreal Canadiens.

Dionne scored 375 points in three seasons with the St. Catherines Black Hawks of the Ontario Hockey Association. He was selected second in the draft by the Detroit Red Wings.

> **Career regular season:**
> 1,348 games, 731 goals, 1,040 assists, 1,771 points
> Two-time winner Lady Byng Trophy (Gentlemanly Play)
> Two-time Ted Lindsay Award winner (Most Outstanding Player)
> One-time Art Ross Trophy winner (High Scorer)
> Two-time first-team NHL All-Star; two-time second-team NHL All-Star
> **Advanced stats: 135.5 OPS, 19.6 DPS, 155.5 PS**
> Elected to Hall of Fame in 1992

Dionne made an immediate impact for the Red Wings with his explosive skating and robust scoring. He tallied 28 goals and 49 assists as a rookie, but that only got him a third-place finish in the rookie of the year voting behind Ken Dryden of the Montreal Canadiens and Rick Martin of the Buffalo Sabres. Lafleur? He did not even finish in the top five in that category.

If Dionne was good as a rookie, he was a full-fledged star in his second season when he notched 40 goals and 50 assists. He was somewhat ordinary in his third year with 78 points, but he became a dominating superstar in 1974–75 when he blasted home 47 goals and his pinpoint passing netted him 74 assists. He also scored a league-record 10 shorthanded goals.

Dionne was on pace to become the next icon for the Red Wings, and if things had worked out, he would have been the player that led the Red Wings to glory.

However, while Detroit management would eventually set the standards for how to run an NHL franchise in the 1990s and beyond, the Red Wings management in the 1970s made a series of poor moves and the team struggled badly. It was time to pay Dionne what he was worth, and the diminutive superstar, at 5-9 and 180 pounds, did not feel like he was getting the respect he deserved from the Red Wings, and he was unhappy with his contract offer.

In those days, there was no free agency that allowed a veteran player to move from his previous team to a new one. Yet Dionne left the Red Wings and signed a free-agency-like deal with the Los Angeles Kings.

Technically, in those days, it wasn't really free agency. The NHL insisted that Detroit needed to get an equitable return for Dionne, and the Kings sent two players and a second-round pick to Detroit for Dionne and another player.

In many ways, it was a great move for Dionne because he was going to a team that recognized his greatness and was willing to pay him well.

However, instead of playing for a beloved team in a great hockey market that would have given him a chance to become a great star outside of the rink, he was going to an area where hockey had very little importance at the time.

Additionally, playing on the West Coast before the era of twenty-four-hour sports coverage meant many fans might only see Dionne play once or twice a year, and the only reason they knew he was a great player was from the scoring he was doing for the Kings that placed him at or near the top of the league's leader board.

Dionne worked hard throughout his 12-year run with the Kings. He scored 50 goals or more five times in Los Angeles, including four seasons in a row from 1978–79 through 1981–82. He scored 100 points or more seven times in a Kings uniform and he tied for the league lead in scoring with 137 points in 1979–80.

But despite those spectacular numbers, Dionne never won the NHL's Hart Trophy that goes to the league's Most Valuable Player. He finished second to Wayne Gretzky in his most explosive scoring year, losing out by 45 votes.

Marcel Dionne

Dionne regularly had to play second-fiddle to Lafleur in the 1970s and Gretzky in the '80s. The Kings became a very competitive and playoff-worthy team during Dionne's run in Los Angeles, but they were not at the championship level.

Those factors all kept Dionne from getting the recognition he arguably should have had during his career. Dionne loved playing for the Kings, but he recognized that hockey did not have the stature in Southern California that came when the team acquired Gretzky and grew even stronger when the team won Stanley Cup championships in 2012 and 2014.

"That was the biggest difference after leaving Detroit," Dionne explained. "There, it's hockey every day. You talk to people. They watch you; they see you. In Los Angeles, once you leave the parking lot of the arena, you're invisible. A lot of guys liked that. I didn't. I like the heat to be on and have people be aware of the team. They were great years, though. It was a great place to play."

The Kings had spectacular success with Dionne centering a line with left wing Charlie Simmer and right wing Dave Taylor. Simmer was a big, powerful forward who loved to station himself in front of the net so he could score on short shots, rebounds, and deflections. Taylor was a great skater and playmaker himself, and he excelled at cashing in on Dionne's feeds.

The Triple Crown line helped put hockey on the map in Los Angeles. Dionne and his linemates were feared and explosive scorers who carried the team to eight playoff seasons.

The Kings never got further than the second round, and he was eventually traded to the New York Rangers for the last two-plus years of his career. While Rangers supporters and Eastern Conference hockey fans did not get to see much of Dionne at the peak of his career, he was often given ovations by fans who knew how great he had been and how much of his career had been played in obscurity.

Dionne was never part of a Stanley Cup winner and never won the MVP Award, but he was a spectacular talent who dominated throughout his eighteen-year career.

#26

Teemu Selanne

Fifteen seasons with Anaheim Ducks. Four seasons with Winnipeg Jets. Three seasons with San Jose Sharks. One season with Colorado Avalanche.

When Teemu Selanne was drafted with the 10th pick in the first round in 1988, there was little question about the Finnish skater's ability to speed up and down the ice, and put the puck in the net. However, with most European players during that era, there was a question about how he would adapt to the North American style of play and the viciousness of the hitting.

There was also the question of when he would come over, because Selanne simply was not ready as an eighteen-year-old to leave home and start playing Canada's tough minor leagues.

Perhaps he could have played right away for the Winnipeg Jets, but that's not how it usually worked. Selanne did not rush things. He stayed in Finland and fulfilled his military commitment and also played for the elite Jokerit team. While playing with seasoned, veteran players, he honed his goal-scoring skills.

> **Career regular season:**
> NHL: 1,451 games, 684 goals, 773 assists, 1,457 points
> One-time Calder Trophy winner (Rookie of the Year)
> One-time Maurice Richard Trophy winner (Leading Goal Scorer)
> One-time Bill Masterton Award winner (Perseverance and Sportsmanship)
> Three-time first-team NHL All-Star; two-time second-team NHL All-Star
> Six-time Stanley Cup winner
> **Advanced stats: 142.9 OPS, 29.4 DPS, 172.3 PS**

When he finally decided to come out and play NHL hockey, he was ready to put his talents on display for the Jets.

Selanne was a flat-out star from the time he started to play for the Jets in the 1992–93 season. Selanne had a rocket of a shot, and the instincts needed to get that shot off with time and space. He scored a record 76 goals and added 56 assists as a rookie.

Prior to Selanne's explosive show, Mike Bossy had held the rookie goal-scoring record with 53 markers in one season. Bossy was one of the greatest scorers the game has ever seen, and Selanne simply obliterated that mark.

Head coach John Paddock was thrilled with the Finnish Flash, and he thought that Selanne "would put hockey back on the map in Winnipeg again."

The 76-goal season was a double-edged sword for Selanne. While it revealed his greatness and unlimited potential, it gave him quite a high standard to live up to.

Selanne remained an explosive player from that point forward, but he never came close to that scoring level again. He reached the 50-goal mark twice in his career, but it was not with the Jets.

Nor did he save hockey in Winnipeg.

Selanne played with the Jets through the midway point of the 1995–96 season, and that's when the struggling Jets traded him to the Mighty Ducks of Anaheim. The Ducks were an improving team that was shedding the expansion label, and having a sniper like Selanne would help them get to a new level.

The Jets? They finished that season in Winnipeg, but that was it for Manitoba. The franchise moved to the desert and became the Phoenix Coyotes. Unhappy Jets fans would rue that day until NHL hockey returned when the Thrashers left Atlanta and moved to Winnipeg prior to the 2011–12 season.

If Selanne had any regrets about leaving his original NHL franchise, it did not show on the ice. Just as he had in his first season in Winnipeg, he brought the house down in his first full season with the Ducks. He scored 51 goals and 58 assists, and he had a knack for scoring when the game was on the line. He tallied eight game-winning goals and he gave the Ducks a credible go-to threat every time he was on the ice in a close game in the third period.

Selanne and the Ducks won a first-round playoff series in 1996–97, beating the Coyotes in seven games. However, they were trounced by the Detroit Red Wings in four games in the next round as the Ducks got an education of what it was like to play a championship team.

It would take a while for those lessons to sink in, but Selanne topped the 50-goal mark for the second year in a row as he scored 52 and established himself as the franchise's go-to scorer.

But it was just not working for the Ducks, and although Selanne was scoring regularly for them, the team decided to make a trade with the San Jose Sharks. The Ducks received Jeff Friesen, goalie Steve Shields, and a draft pick for Selanne.

Teemu Selanne

After playing one-and-a-half seasons for the Sharks, Selanne signed a one-year free-agent contract with the Colorado Avalanche, and that did not work out well. After scoring just 16 goals and 16 assists for the Avs, Selanne was once again a free agent, and he returned home to the Ducks in 2005–06. He flourished in Anaheim, scoring 40 goals and 50 assists, and he helped the Mighty Ducks advance past the Calgary Flames and the Colorado Avalanche in the Western Conference playoffs before they were stopped by the Edmonton Oilers.

Selanne had his best playoff performance, scoring six goals and eight assists in 16 games.

The next season they became the Anaheim Ducks, and the change suited them well, because the Ducks had a powerhouse season in 2010, as they won the Pacific Division with 110 points and were second in the Western Conference to the Detroit Red Wings.

The Ducks overpowered the Minnesota Wild and the Vancouver Canucks, while the Red Wings downed the Flames and the Sharks. That set up an epic confrontation between the West's two best teams.

While most expected the veteran and seasoned Red Wings to roll, the Ducks were tough and explosive with Selanne, Scott Niedermayer, Chris Pronger, Andy McDonald, and young Ryan Getzlaf. The Ducks handled the Red Wings in six games and moved to the Stanley Cup Final against the Ottawa Senators.

The Sens were tough and feisty, but they could not match the Ducks' power, explosiveness, and talent. Anaheim won in five games, and hoisted the Stanley Cup. The sharpshooting Selanne had 48 goals that season.

He continued to play productive hockey through the 2011–12 season before he finally called it a career.

He might have slowed his last two years, but by the time he hung up his skates, Selanne had lit the lamp 684 times.

He would never again score at the explosive level he did during his rookie season, but he will always be remembered as one of the greatest goal scorers of all-time.

#27

Martin Brodeur

Twenty-one seasons with New Jersey Devils. One season with St. Louis Blues.

W as Martin Brodeur the best goalie in the history of the National Hockey League? A look at the record book reveals that there is no doubt about his dominance.

He is the all-time leader in wins (691), regular-season shutouts (125), playoff shutouts (24), most 40-win seasons (8), most 30-win seasons (12), and he was the youngest goalie to reach 300, 400, and 500 victories.

Martin Brodeur

Brodeur was the back-stop of a New Jersey Devils team that won three Stanley Cups during his brilliant run. He stayed a Devil throughout all but the last days of his career, and he was the perfect goalie for a team that had made defense its top priority. Interestingly, Brodeur loved scoring goals in his youth. Like most Canadian youngsters, he was on skates from about the time he could walk, and he played forward in his very early days. However, when he started to compete in tournaments and leagues at the age of seven, his coach came up to him and asked him if he wanted to play forward or goalie.

Career regular season:
NHL Career: 1266 games, 691-397-154, 2.24 goals-against average, .912 save percentage, 125 shutouts
One-time Calder Trophy winner (Rookie of the Year)
Four-time Vezina Trophy winner (Top Goaltender)
Five-time William Jennings Trophy winner (Fewest Goals Allowed)
Three-time first-team NHL All-Star. Four-time second-team NHL All-Star
Three-time Stanley Cup winner

Like most seven-year-olds, Brodeur made his decision on what sounded like the most fun. "It was the most important decision of my life, and I made it as a seven-year-old," Brodeur said in an interview with the Hockey Hall of Fame. "I just thought it would be fun to play goalie."

Not only did it turn out to be the right decision, it was brilliant. Brodeur was perhaps the last of the league's elite stand-up goalies. Most netminders who came along at the same time as Brodeur in the 1993–94 season would flop to the ice in order to make stops, and by the late 1990s, nearly all of them did.

Brodeur remained true to his style throughout his career, because that's how he was comfortable playing. There may have been some hiccups as he worked his way up to the NHL, but by the time team president/general manager Lou Lamoriello promoted him full-time to the varsity, he was ready to give the Devils their most consistent goaltending performance since Sean Burke was between the pipes.

Brodeur had plenty of assets in the net. He challenged shooters by coming out of the crease and cutting down on the angle and he had tremendous mobility going from post to post. He was big and made himself look big in goal by spreading out as much as he could before opposing forwards and defensemen took their shots. He was also an outstanding skater and puck handler, and that saved his team from handling too many scoring opportunities.

When the Devils named Jacques Lemaire as their head coach prior to the 1993–94 season, the die was cast. Lemaire had been a brilliant but underrated center throughout his Hall of Fame career with the Montreal Canadiens, and he often made his biggest plays dishing the puck to Guy Lafleur. However, while he had excellent offensive skills, he always thought defense first and tried to play a responsible game.

He instilled this in his team and the Devils got the lesson very well. Brodeur made a big impact in Lemaire's first season with a 2.40 goals-against average and a .915 save percentage along with the first three shutouts of his career.

The Devils were good enough to make the playoffs that season, and Brodeur upped his game in the postseason. He had a 1.95 GAA and a .928 save percentage as the Devils beat the Buffalo Sabres and Boston Bruins in the first two rounds of the playoffs.

The upstart Devils met the favored New York Rangers in the Eastern Conference Final, and the upset was nearly complete as they went home for Game 6 with a 3-2 lead in the series. The Rangers were desperately looking for a spark, and they got it when Mark Messier guaranteed a victory.

Messier scored a hat trick for New York to even the series, and the seventh game, played at Madison Square Garden, was a double overtime classic. Stephane Matteau skated behind the net with the puck and suddenly darted out and tried to shovel the puck off of Brodeur and into the net. The goal propelled the Rangers to the Stanley Cup and ended the Devils' season, but it was a play that would propel Brodeur to greatness.

He may have been beaten by the Rangers in that series, but he spent the large majority of his career frustrating the Original Six team.

Martin Brodeur

Brodeur and the Devils did not remain frustrated for very long. They won the Stanley Cup in 1994–95, and Brodeur was absolutely brilliant during the run. He had a 16-4 record, a 1.67 GAA, and a .927 save percentage.

The Devils were merely a third-place team in the Atlantic Division in the lockout-shortened regular season, but there was nothing mediocre about their playoff performance in 1995. The rolled over the Bruins and Penguins in the first two rounds, beating both teams in five games. They had their biggest test in the Eastern Conference Final against the Flyers, but they got rid of Philadelphia in six games.

They were expected to have their hands filled with the Detroit Red Wings in the Stanley Cup Final, but the Devils swept them in four games as Brodeur held them to two goals or less in all four games.

Brodeur led the Devils to Stanley Cups in 1999–2000 and 2002–03. In the 2000 Stanley Cup run, he had a 1.61 GAA and a .927 save percentage as the Devils beat the Dallas Stars in the Stanley Cup Final, while he registered a 1.65 GAA and a .934 save percentage and had seven brilliant shutouts in 2003 as the Devils outlasted the Mighty Ducks of Anaheim in the Stanley Cup Final.

Brodeur also had a close call that could have resulted in a fourth Stanley Cup. The Devils got to the Stanley Cup Final in the 2000–01 season against the Colorado Avalanche and they had earned a 3-2 lead after five games.

The Avalanche were desperate to win the series for defenseman Ray Bourque, who had never won the cup in his long and brilliant career and had moved to Colorado in 2000 in a last-ditch effort to bring it home. Bourque led the Avs to a win in Game 6 on the road, and the Avs closed the series out at home.

It was the most disappointing moment of Brodeur's career. "To get that close and not bring it home hurts," Brodeur said. "The Avalanche had a great team and they earned it, but we had our chance."

Brodeur gave the Devils a chance to win on most nights throughout his career. He is statistically the best goalie who ever played the game, and there is no doubt that he has earned his status among the elite.

#28

Chris Chelios

Seven seasons with Montreal Canadiens. Nine seasons with Chicago Black-hawks. Ten seasons with Detroit Red Wings. One season with Atlanta Thrashers.

The great irony of Chris Chelios's memorable career is that it almost never happened at all.

Chelios began playing in the NHL in the 1983–84 season with the Montreal Canadiens, and he didn't complete his career until 2009–10 when he was a forty-eight-year-old graybeard with the Atlanta Thrashers. When it comes to longevity and getting the most out of his body, Chelios belongs in a category with the great Gordie Howe and nobody else.

But as a youngster, Chelios was anything but the dominating defenseman he would be for the majority of his career. He could not make his college hockey team, and then failed in two separate attempts to make Junior B teams in Canada.

> **Career regular season:**
> 1,681 games, 185 goals, 763 assists, 948 points
> Three-time Norris Trophy winner (Best Defenseman)
> Six-time first-team NHL All-Star; two-time second-team NHL All-Star
> Three-time Stanley Cup winner
> **Advanced stats: 59.8 OPS, 108.6 DPS, 168.4 PS**
> Elected to Hall of Fame in 2013

Chelios refused to take no for an answer. He returned home to California, spent an offseason getting bigger and stronger in the weight room, and then earned a spot with the Moose Jaw Canucks of the Saskatchewan Junior Hockey League.

Chelios made the most of his opportunity, and he was noticed by the Canadiens, who drafted him with a second-round pick in 1981. After getting his feet wet in his first season with the team, he became a legitimate starter in his second year and it was clear he was going to become a formidable player. Chelios scored nine goals and 55 assists in 1984–85, but more than the numbers, Chelios played with an edge that bordered between mean and vicious.

Go into the corners with Chelios, and he was going to come away with the puck and his opponent was likely to come away with a significant dose of pain. Whether it was from a shoulder, elbow, or the well-placed butt of his stick, Chelios didn't care. He was going to do whatever it took to win that battle and help his team win the game.

Chelios would help the Habs win an unexpected Stanley Cup in the 1985–86 playoffs. That was the season that goalie Patrick Roy made his debut, and he gave the underdog Habs a chance to win every time they stepped on the ice. While the Canadiens may not have had their most physically gifted team that season, they did have a bunch of junkyard dog-type players who would attack every opportunity they had and find a way to win games against more talented opponents.

Chelly was a big part of that team, with two goals and nine assists during the 20-game playoff run, and he also had 49 penalty minutes during that run.

Chelios only got better from that point as he continued to establish himself as a hard-hitting, powerful defenseman. He would reach a new level of success during the 1988–89 season when he became an offensive threat every time he stepped onto the ice. Chelios scored 15 goals and 58 assists for the Habs, and that performance allowed him to gain first-team All-Star status and earned him the first of his three Norris Trophies.

That was quite an achievement because Boston's Ray Bourque was considered the NHL's best and most consistent defenseman, and to take that award away from him was considered quite incredible.

Chelios was a star for the Montreal Canadiens, but he was traded to Chicago after the 1989–90 season. The trade was a dream come true for Chelios, who was born and raised in Evergreen Park, Illinois, which was just a stone's throw away from the Chicago Stadium.

The Blackhawks had been the team that Chelios had rooted for growing up, so this homecoming had real meaning to him.

While the Blackhawks were not perennial contenders, they were an up-and-coming team prior to the 1990–91 season. They had a chance to win the team's first Stanley Cup in thirty-one years during Chelios's second season with the team, but the Blackhawks were unable to contain the powerful Pittsburgh Penguins with Mario Lemieux and Jaromir Jagr. Chicago lost that series in four straight games.

Nevertheless, Chelios was in the prime of his career during his eight years with the Blackhawks, as he was a two-time Norris Trophy winner, a three-time first-team All-Star, and a second-team All-Star once. Chelios played heavy minutes for the Blackhawks, and he helped give his hometown team a tough and unrelenting identity.

Chelios was known for his work ethic and conditioning throughout his career, and as he reached his mid-thirties, he knew that he was still capable of playing in the National Hockey League. However, the Blackhawks saw his career in the ending stages, and they let Chelios know that the team had a job for him in the front office when his career came to an end.

Chelios understood that the Blackhawks were giving him a not-so-gentle hint about where they saw his future, and he let the team know that he was not ready to retire.

He had said during the last few years of his career in Chicago that he wanted to retire as a Blackhawk, but that meant when he was ready to give up playing and hang up his skates. He didn't care if others thought he should fade off into the sunset, because he was a competitor who had more to give even if the calendar said it was time to retire or give strong consideration to the notion.

The Blackhawks traded Chelios to the Detroit Red Wings in 1999. They thought he was an aging player with waning skills, but Chelios knew that was not the case and the Blackhawks' rivals knew it as well.

The trade left a bad taste in many fans' mouths because Chelios was a hometown guy. They couldn't believe he would willingly suit up for the Red Wings and they resented him for it.

They shouldn't have. That's the way professional sports is, and Chelios had every right to continue playing as long as he could and as long as a team was willing to pay for his services.

That turned out to be nine more full seasons plus a portion of one more year. Chelios was a lot more than just a functional NHL player. He was a first-team NHL all-star at the age of forty, and he finished second in the Norris Trophy voting.

Chelios was also a part of two more Stanley Cup-winning teams with the Red Wings. His last season in Detroit was the 2008–09 season, and while he was playing on fumes at that point as the NHL's second-oldest competitor behind Gordie Howe, he remained a physical force until the end.

"I feel so fortunate to have an opportunity again at my age. In my wildest dreams, never, if you asked me 10 years ago, [did I think] I'd still be playing at this level," Chelios said when he finally called it a career following the 2009–10 season.

Considering his halting start, it was an amazing career that few could ever have imagined.

#29

Johnny Bucyk

Twenty-one seasons with Boston Bruins. Two seasons with Detroit Red Wings.

The Big Bad Boston Bruins of the late 1960s and early 1970s were basically a young, swashbuckling team that marauded its way through the competition.

Roaring and fun-loving, they knew how to tend to business when the puck was dropped. But if there were ever any shaky moments that required leadership, the young Bruins looked to veteran Johnny Bucyk to show them the way.

Career regular season:
1,540 games, 566 goals, 813 assists, 1,369 points
Two-time Lady Byng Trophy winner (Gentlemanly Play)
One-time first-team NHL All-Star; one-time second-team NHL All-Star
Two-time Stanley Cup champion
Advanced stats: 104.0 OPS, 18.3 DPS, 122.3 PS
Elected to Hall of Fame in 1981

By the time the Bruins had emerged as a force in the NHL, Bucyk had already been through the wars. He played his first two seasons with Detroit, and was traded to the Bruins prior to the 1957–58 season where he played on a line with Vic Stasiuk and Bronco Horvath. While the Bruins would not enjoy many good seasons during the early part of Bucyk's tenure with the team, they got to the Stanley Cup Finals that year and extended the Montreal Canadiens to six games before finally falling short.

"The Chief" was a consistent goal scorer, averaging 22 goals for a team that struggled through much of his first nine seasons with the squad.

However, the Bruins began to turn the corner in 1966–67 when Bobby Orr arrived. The scintillating defenseman gave the Bruins a remarkable star who was capable of making the fans hold their breath every time he got the puck—and also capable of doing the same thing to players on both teams.

Orr was a young phenom when he put on a Bruins uniform in 1966–67, and the Bruins management had high hopes that he would transform them into a championship team. But they also knew he was an eighteen-year-old when he came to the team, with a teenager's view of the world. The Bruins assigned Bucyk to be Orr's roommate so he could show the youngster the ropes.

There was no hazing or any other typical jocular routine with the Bruins and Orr. Bucyk wouldn't allow it. He knew his job was to do everything he could to prepare Orr for the rigorous ordeal of the NHL season and he handled the job well.

Johnny Bucyk

"We talked often and his words meant a lot to me then as they do now," Orr said in his 2014 autobiography, *Orr My Story*. "Johnny was a great help to me in making the transition from junior hockey to the pros."

The Bruins became known for their high-scoring and spectacular games during their run up the NHL ladder. However, while Orr and stars like Phil Esposito, Ken Hodge, and Wayne Cashman became headline players, Bucyk was the steady, blue-collar worker who provided a consistent effort every game and was one of the team's most dependable players.

He scored 30 goals in 1967–68, 24 in '68-69, and 31 in '69-70. The Bruins were playoff teams in each of those years. They fell to Montreal in the 1968 playoffs, but were much improved the following year. They routed Toronto in four games in '69 before falling to the Canadiens in six games. However, the next year there was no stopping the Bruins.

They beat a New York Rangers team in six games, and swept the Chicago Blackhawks in four games to get to the Stanley Cup Finals against the St. Louis Blues.

The Blues were a third-year expansion team that season, and they went to the Finals in each of their two previous seasons. They had been swept by Montreal both of their first two seasons, and while they were clear underdogs against Boston, their previous experience meant that they were not nervous about playing in the Finals.

But they were overmatched. The Bruins offense scored at will, and Bucyk was often in the middle of most of the damage. Bucyk and his linemates Fred Stanfield and Johnny "Pie" McKenzie threw the puck around with ease and they were able to torment the St. Louis defense at will. The Bruins swept the series and raised the Stanley Cup for the first time since 1941.

Bucyk played in 14 playoff games that year, and he scored 11 goals and eight assists during that memorable championship run.

Many thought the Bruins would become the league's next dynasty after they won that Stanley Cup, and they had a dominating regular season in 1970–71. They rampaged through the league and finished first in the Eastern Conference with a 57–14–7 record.

They scored 399 goals in 78 games, and it was not unusual for the Bruins to score six, seven, or eight goals in any game. Bucyk was one of many beneficiaries of the team's high-scoring ways. He scored a career-high 51 goals and 65 assists, and his ability to maneuver the puck when he was close to the net allowed him to become a dominant player.

Bucyk was shocked as to how the season had gone for him. He had never scored more than 31 goals and 69 points in a season. He knew he was on a powerful team and had hoped to score 38 goals that season. He went flying by that mark with ease.

Bucyk had scored 49 goals when the Bruins went into Detroit in March of 1971, and he hoped that would be the night he reached 50. He went in with Stanfield on a 2-on-1, and when his linemate shot the puck and Detroit goalie Roy Edwards kicked out a rebound, Bucyk jumped on it and flipped it into the top corner of the net.

The Bruins were expected to repeat their championship run in the playoffs, but Montreal rookie goaltender Ken Dryden dominated the series and the Habs beat the Bruins in seven games to shock the hockey world.

The embarrassed Bruins came back the following year and regained their championship form. They rolled past Toronto and St. Louis in the first two rounds, and met the hated New York Rangers in the Stanley Cup Finals.

The two teams were both talented and powerful, but the Bruins had Orr and were the more explosive offensive team. Boston won the series in six games, and Bucyk was able to skate around Madison Square Garden with the Stanley Cup.

Bucyk would play six more seasons with the Bruins, and as he reached his late thirties, he was no longer the skater that he had been in his early years. However, he remained a talented scorer because he went to the front of the net and he was able to draw opposing goalies out of position and then finish his scoring attempts.

Johnny Bucyk

He called it a career after the 1977–78 season, and he has remained a vital part of the Bruins' organization since then. There may not be a bronze statue of Bucyk in front of the TD Garden like there is of Orr, but he is the quintessential Bruin whose loyalty and productivity remain his calling cards.

#30

Gilbert Perreault

Seventeen seasons with Buffalo Sabres.

What does it take to turn a team into a contender?

Does it take years of hard work by scouts to find players in the draft and a savvy general manager who can raid opponents' rosters and make important trades?

Sometimes, it takes years to overcome the inertia that comes with losing consistently. But it's not always so complicated.

Find the right player at the right time, and a team can become dangerous seemingly overnight.

Gilbert Perreault

That was the story with Gilbert Perreault when he was drafted by the expansion Buffalo Sabres prior to the 1970-71 season.

That was the first year the Sabres started playing in the NHL, coming in the same year as the Vancouver Canucks. Not much was expected from either of those teams, because they were only able to choose from the left-overs that the twelve established NHL

> **Career regular season:**
> 1,191 games, 512 goals, 814 assists, 1,326 points
> One-time Calder Trophy winner (Rookie of the Year)
> One-time Lady Byng Memorial Trophy winner (Gentlemanly Play)
> Two-time second-team NHL All-Star
> **Advanced stats: 96.0 OPS, 17.3 DPS, 113.3 PS**
> Elected to Hall of Fame in 1990

teams did not choose to protect. But while the Canucks were picking up Orland Kurtenbach in the expansion draft and the Sabres were doing the same with Don Luce, one of those teams was about to hit it big.

The Sabres and Canucks were given the first two spots in the NHL's player draft that season, and a coin toss would determine which team would select first. Punch Imlach, the first general manager of the Sabres, got lucky when a spin of the wheel of fortune came up with a Sabres logo on it.

Imlach drafted Perreault, who had been a record-setting performer with the Montreal Junior Canadiens in 1969 and '70. He had led his team to back-to-back national championships and had been named the MVP in the Ontario Hockey Association.

He was the best young amateur player in the world and clearly worthy of the No. 1 spot in the draft. Perreault proved worthy of the selection when he scored 38 goals and 34 assists for the expansion Sabres as a rookie.

Perreault credited the demanding Imlach with helping make him an explosive offensive player. "In my first seasons, Imlach told me to go for goals and not worry about checking," Perreault said.

"That really helped me get my confidence. The first few years I was there, it was loose [offensively]. I was rushing the puck a lot. We had style."

Buffalo struggled to win games in the team's first year, but any hockey fan who saw the Sabres play that year realized that the Sabres were no ordinary expansion team. Perreault had exceptional skating ability, brilliant hockey instincts, and the ability to take over any game.

He did not have the kind of teammates around him who could take advantage of his pinpoint passing and playmaking ability, but there were some nights during that rookie year when Perreault did remarkable things on his own. He could skate through the neutral zone with speed, stop on a dime, and start up again to create his own scoring opportunity.

Imlach, one of the smartest executives in the game, knew that the presence of Perreault gave him a player who was capable of carrying an expansion team on his back and making them respectable. However, he realized if he could get Perreault a few more talented teammates, the Sabres would not be an "expansion" team for very long. They were capable of making the playoffs and becoming dangerous contenders.

That's what happened when the Sabres drafted a dangerous scorer in Richard Martin and acquired previously unheralded Rene Robert from the Pittsburgh Penguins. Sabres head coach Floyd Smith had Perreault center the Sabres' top line with Martin at left wing and Robert on the right side, and the team became one of the most explosive offensive units in the league.

Buffalo quickly became a feared team because of the "French Connection" line. The Sabres made the playoffs in the 1972–73 season, and while they lost their first-round matchup with the Montreal Canadiens in six games, it was clear that the Sabres would be a force in the upcoming seasons.

Perreault spearheaded their rise. His performance during his rookie season was good enough to win him the rookie of the year award, and he quickly followed with 74 points in his second season and 88 in 1972-73.

Gilbert Perreault

Injuries limited Perreault to 55 games in 1973–74 and also knocked the Sabres out of the playoffs, but a healthy Perreault returned the following year and the Sabres were on top of their game throughout the season.

Perreault was especially sharp, as he seemed both faster and stronger than he had ever been. He scored 39 goals and added 57 assists, and he was virtually unstoppable when the game was on the line in the third period.

The Sabres were remarkable that year, finishing the regular season with a 49-16-15 record, and their 113 points allowed them to finish in first place in the NHL's Adams Division by a whopping 19 points over the veteran Boston Bruins.

It only got better in the postseason, as the Sabres did not even have to play in the NHL's preliminary round because their division championship gave them a pass to the second round. They dispatched the veteran Chicago Blackhawks easily, beating them by a 4-1 margin.

The bubble was expected to burst in the following round against Montreal, but the Sabres did not appear the least bit intimidated by the NHL's most decorated franchise. Instead, they whipped the Habs in six games.

That earned the Sabres a spot in the Stanley Cup Finals against the Philadelphia Flyers, who were the league's defending champions. Few gave the Sabres a chance in the series against the Broad Street Bullies, who had beaten Bobby Orr and the Bruins in the championship round the season before.

The Flyers were the most intimidating team in the league. However, after dropping the first two games of the series in Philadelphia, the Sabres bounced back with wins in Games 3 and 4 in Buffalo.

Game 3 was one of the most famous games in Stanley Cup Final history. The ancient Buffalo Memorial Auditorium was not air-conditioned, and 90-degree temperatures caused fog to shroud the ice.

Throughout the game—and especially in the later stages—maintenance workers had to come out onto the ice and skate around with bed sheets to help dissipate the fog.

The Sabres tied the game late in the third period, and then won it in overtime when Martin passed to Perreault. As he crossed the blue line, he dished a pass to Robert. The right wing fired a quick shot through the fog that got through Philadelphia goaltender Bernie Parent for the winning goal.

The "Fog Game" would go on to live forever in NHL annals.

The Sabres could not sustain their success and succumbed in six games, but nobody could slow down Perreault during that playoff year. He scored six goals and nine assists in 17 games, and four of his goals came on the power play. No matter what the Blackhawks, Canadiens, or Flyers did, Perreault kept piling up the points and creating scoring opportunities.

The Sabres never got back to the championship round in any of Perreault's remaining seasons, but he was a dominant player for nearly all of his seventeen seasons in Buffalo.

He stayed with the Sabres throughout his career, and he remains the greatest player in the history of the franchise.

#31

Brad Park

Eight seasons with Boston Bruins. Eight seasons with New York Rangers. Two seasons with Detroit Red Wings.

Forever just a brief shining moment, there was Camelot.

The romantic notion is often associated with the tragically short presidency of John F. Kennedy. When the thirty-fifth president inhabited the White House with his wife Jackie Kennedy and his two young children, those early years in the 1960s were often referred to as America's version of Camelot.

Career regular season:

1,113 games, 213 goals, 683 assists, 896 points

One-time Bill Masterton Trophy winner (Perseverance and Sportsmanship)

Four-time first-team NHL All-Star; two time second-team NHL All-Star

Advanced stats: 66.3 OPS, 76.9 DPS, 143.2 PS

Elected to Hall of Fame in 1988

But there was a Camelot associated with the NHL, and it was far shorter than the nearly three years Kennedy was in the White House.

It was a period of 10 games when Bobby Orr and Brad Park were in the Boston Bruins lineup together.

That's all it lasted, but what a time it was when Orr and Park played together in Boston.

Orr was the brilliant leader of the Bruins and perhaps the most spectacular talent to ever play the game. Park was his greatest rival, and he excelled for the New York Rangers while Orr was writing history for the New York Rangers.

In nearly any other era, a great argument could have been made that Park was the best defenseman of his generation. But since he came up just two years after Orr, Park could never make that claim.

Park played spectacularly for the Rangers, and he gave the team something it had rarely seen before his arrival in 1968–69. Park was a defenseman who could skate with the puck, create plays, and come through with a goal or a pass that set one up at the most important moment.

He played the same style of game for the Rangers as Orr did for the Bruins. However, while Park was a sharp decision maker and could see the game nearly as well as Orr and was just as important to New York as Orr was to Boston, the Rangers' defenseman could not match Orr when it came to explosive speed.

Park could certainly move well enough and better than most defensemen, but he could not move the puck at the warp speed of his competitor, and it was one of the reasons that he could not claim equal status.

Brad Park

While Orr was winning the Norris Trophy nearly every year, Park finished as the runner-up for that honor six times.

If the presence of Orr frustrated Park, he never let it out. Actually, he was far too smart for that. Orr had been in the league a couple of seasons by the time Park played his rookie season with the Rangers, and he tried to improve his game by studying Orr's game.

"Bobby had a definite influence on my play," Park told the Hockey Hall of Fame. "I began studying him during the 1968–69 season. While I was recuperating from my broken ankle, I got a chance to watch Bobby a bit closer in a couple of games on television and a couple more in person. I'll tell you this, he slowed things down and when he suckered somebody in, he'd burst around them with his fantastic accelerations."

Park quickly became a star with the Rangers. He was a first-team All-Star with New York in his second season, and he remained a first- or second-team All-Star for the next four seasons as well.

As Park thrived, so did the Rangers. They became a perennial playoff team, and Park was the defenseman that head coach Emile Francis had on the ice in nearly all crucial situations.

The Rangers came close to the Stanley Cup Final or winning it all in 1971, 1972, and 1974, but they were stopped by teams like the Chicago Blackhawks, the Bruins and the Philadelphia Flyers in heartbreaking playoff losses.

Park's best season with the Rangers came in 1973–74 when he scored 24 goals and 57 assists. The Rangers got to the semifinal round of the playoffs that year and extended Philadelphia to seven games, but the Rangers came up short in the decisive contest.

The Rangers never got in sync in 1974–75, and they were upset in the first round of the playoffs by the New York Islanders. This rubbed management the wrong way, and the team got rid of beloved goaltender Ed Giacomin and traded Park and center Jean Ratelle to the Bruins for Phil Esposito.

None of the major participants were happy at first, and Park even considered hanging up his skates so he didn't have to play for a team that he despised.

That thought lasted just a few moments. The Bruins wanted Park because they knew that Orr's knees were shot and that he couldn't last much longer. However, they did play together for a short time, and it was brilliant to watch the two All-Stars play with each other. While Orr's speed was down and his pain tolerance was up, his instincts were still razor-sharp and playing with Park was good for him.

Eventually, Orr couldn't lace up his skates and play any longer. That left Park as the Bruins' top defenseman, and the transition to Boston that he feared would go badly turned out to be one of the best things for his career.

Instead of treating him like an outsider, the Bruins welcomed Park like a long-lost brother. "Johnny Bucyk, in particular, was very helpful. Bobby Orr was just super, as a person as well as a player," Park said. "All the so-called knowledgeable hockey people were saying that New York got the best of the deal, so I just had to go out and show Boston fans that they got the best of it."

Park wondered what would happen with his first visit back to Madison Square Garden. He was shocked when Rangers fans booed him, because he had played his heart out for eight years. He got even more upset because Bruins fans welcomed Esposito with an ovation on his first trip back to Boston.

Park used that as motivation, and he played stellar hockey for Bruins coach Don Cherry. Park's best season in Boston may have been 1977–78, when he scored 22 goals and 57 assists. The Bruins got to the Stanley Cup Final that year against the Montreal Canadiens, but they lost to the Habs in six games.

That marked the third time in Park's career—once with the Rangers and twice with the Bruins—that his team got to the Final. His teams lost each time.

There was no shame in losing in '77 and '78 to the Canadiens, since Scotty Bowman's team may have been the best in NHL history.

Still Park played eight seasons with the Rangers, eight with the Bruins, and two with the Detroit Red Wings, and he never won the Stanley Cup.

Brad Park

That's the big regret in his stellar career, but it didn't prevent him from becoming one of the greatest defensemen the game has ever known.

"I played on some great teams, but we got beat by some better ones," Park said. "I would have loved to have won the Stanley Cup, but it was not in the cards."

#32

Brett Hull

Two seasons with Calgary Flames. Eleven seasons with St. Louis Blues. Three seasons with Dallas Stars. Three seasons with Detroit Red Wings. One season with Phoenix Coyotes.

Brett Hull came into the NHL with a familiar name and look to hockey fans. His father, Bobby Hull, was one of the NHL's most visible stars of the 1960s and '70s and his booming slapshot changed the sport dramatically.

Brett Hull was met with equal parts of skepticism and enthusiasm. The skeptics believed that his father's huge impact could easily

Brett Hull

overwhelm the son and that he would drown in a sea of high expectations. The enthusiasts could see that Brett was special in his own right and would be able to forge his own name and become a great player in the NHL.

In most of life, it seems the skeptics usually win out as high expectations and pressure are capable of overpowering the most gifted athletes. In Brett Hull's case, they certainly did not.

He forged his own

> **Career regular season:**
> 1,269 games, 741 goals, 650 assists, 1,391 points
> One-time Lady Bing Trophy winner (Gentlemanly Play)
> One-time Hart Trophy winner (MVP)
> One-time Ted Lindsay Award winner (Outstanding Offensive Player)
> Three-time first-team NHL All-Star
> Two-time Stanley Cup winner
> Elected to Hall of Fame in 2009
> **Advanced stats: 134.3 OPS, 20.3 DPS, 156.6 PS**

name, played to a level of greatness that nobody could have predicted, and was in many ways like his father.

Bobby Hull may have had the most dominating slapshot of any player who has ever competed in the NHL, but Brett Hull may have had the best wrist shot ever. That's really an amazing dichotomy for father and son, as each is atop his own (subjective) category of hockey greatness.

It didn't start out that way for the younger Hull, because he was unimpressive as a junior hockey player—he was somewhat overweight and did not have a reputation as a hard worker. After playing at the Junior B level, he spent two years playing college hockey at Minnesota-Duluth. Hull was an eye-opening scorer with 105 goals in 56 games.

Despite that impressive production, he wasn't drafted until the sixth round when the Calgary Flames selected him with the 117th pick overall. The Flames brought him up to the NHL in the 1986–87 season, but he didn't play regularly until the next year. He scored

26 goals through 52 games, and that's when the Flames traded him to the St. Louis Blues.

The Blues figured Hull would give them consistent scoring, but they couldn't have had any idea that he would become a dominant figure who would turn out to be one of the most explosive scorers the game has ever seen.

Hull scored 41 goals and 43 assists in 1988–89 with the Blues, and that was his first full season with the team. However, he raised it up another two or three levels in 1989–90 when he became the league's dominant goal scorer with 72 markers. He also had 41 assists and earned the Lady Byng Trophy and finished third among Hart Trophy contenders.

There would be no third-place finish the following year. Nearly everything that Hull touched went in the back of the net as he scored an incredible 86 goals and 45 assists. Wayne Gretzky is the only player who has scored more goals in a season, as he had 92 in 1981–82, and he also had 87 in 1983–84.

But Hull's back-to-back seasons of 72 and 86 goals left no doubt that he had fully emerged from his father's huge shadow and was carving his own individual legacy in the NHL.

Hull's wrist shot was a sight to behold. Even though he was not the biggest player at 5-11 and 205 pounds, he whipped his shots off of his stick with incredible torque that made it very difficult for opposing goaltenders to follow. He would also get rid of his snap shots so quickly that they would seem to be on the goaltender before he could react.

The slapshot? That was basically his father's device and Brett rarely went to it. When he did, it was good, but it was the wrist shot and snap shot that allowed him to torment goalies all over the league.

Hull was clearly becoming one of the top goal scorers in NHL history, and the Blues helped him get there when they acquired center Adam Oates. They placed Hull and Oates on a line together, and it seemed the more Hull shot, the more often the precise Oates would get him the puck and put it in a spot where he could fire rockets.

"It was just a great partnership," Hull said. "Adam was simply one of the best centers in hockey and just an incredible passer. I was a shooter and he had the ability to get me the puck in a place I could handle it well and get my shot off quickly. As a goal scorer, I couldn't ask for more."

Hull had another dominating season in 1991–92 with 70 goals, but his partnership with Oates came to an end when the center was traded to the Boston Bruins. Hull was not pleased, and while he would play with the Blues for another six seasons, he would eventually sign a free-agent contract with the Dallas Stars.

Hull had been very close to signing with the Chicago Blackhawks, his father's old team, but the Dallas offer was just too overwhelming to refuse.

In addition to that, the Stars were an improving team and getting close to the Stanley Cup. The addition of Hull may have been the key move in the development of a team that already had Mike Modano and Joe Nieuwendyk. The Stars got to the Stanley Cup Final, where they would meet a very feisty and aggressive team in the Buffalo Sabres.

The Stars took a 3-2 lead into Game 6 in Buffalo, and Sabres goalie Dominik Hasek was bound and determined to keep the Stars from winning on his team's home ice. The teams battled into triple overtime tied at 1-1, before Hull jumped on a loose puck that was sitting in front of the goalie and banged it into the net for the Stanley Cup.

However, the front of Hull's left foot was in the crease, and according to the letter of the NHL's rules at that time, the goal could have been disallowed.

But that did not happen and while Hull and his teammates rejoiced, Sabres fans remain bitter about the non-call to this day.

Hull would win another Stanley Cup in the latter portion of his career with the Detroit Red Wings, and he would be a productive scorer through the 2003–04 season when he recorded 25 goals and 43 assists.

After the NHL lost the 2004–05 season due to its lockout of the players, Hull tried a brief comeback with the Phoenix Coyotes, but he put an end to that trial after failing to score a goal in five games.

Still, Hull exceeded all expectations throughout his career and became one of the most productive players in NHL history.

#33

Jari Kurri

Ten years with Edmonton Oilers. Five years with Los Angeles Kings. One year with Anaheim Mighty Ducks. One year with Colorado Avalanche. One year with New York Rangers.

He had the good fortune to play the large majority of his career as Wayne Gretzky's right-hand man, but don't think for a second that Kurri was not a very special player all on his own.

The first truly great Finnish import to play in the NHL was a terrific hockey player with a blistering wrist shot and superb passing ability, and he was also one of the finest defensive forwards in the NHL.

Career regular season:

1,251 games, 601 goals, 797 assists, 1,398 points

One-time Lady Byng Trophy winner (Gentlemanly Play)

Two-time first-team NHL All-Star; three-time second-team NHL All-Star

Five-time Stanley Cup champion

Elected to Hall of Fame in 2001

Advanced stats: 98.7 OPS, 18.6 DPS, 117.3 PS

Kurri's responsibility on the defensive end not only broke up many opponents' offensive thrusts, but it also started many plays for the Edmonton Oilers and Los Angeles Kings. Kurri had the ability to turn defense into offense in an instant, and that helped to make both of those teams very dangerous.

Kurri joined the Oilers in 1980–81, and he was not sure the NHL was going to be anything more than a pit stop. He originally planned to play in North America for two or three years before going back to Finland.

There was no indication that his plans would change early in that season, as head coach Glen Sather was not sure which line to play him on. But when Gretzky's line was not operating at peak efficiency with Blair McDonald at right wing, Sather decided to give his reluctant Finnish right wing a shot at playing with the Great One.

There was almost no getting-acquainted period between the two stars. Both players had very strong seasons, but Kurri's rookie year was not an easy one.

"I had tough times in my first year," Kurri said. "I had 17 games without a goal playing with Wayne [Gretzky]. It wasn't easy to go through that with the media, night after night. I had some tough times."

But the difficulties did not last very long.

Kurri scored 32 goals in each of his first two years with the Oilers, but that was just a jumping off point for him. He potted 45 goals in 1982–83 and then became the first Finnish player to exceed the 50-goal mark in the NHL when he scored 52 times the following year.

Kurri was amazingly accurate with his shot. He scored on 26.8 percent of his shots on net in 1983–84, and he stayed in that range for each of the next two seasons. While opponents gave him more room than other right wings of his quality would get because of Gretzky's presence, Kurri simply excelled at putting the puck in the net by hitting the far corners.

By the 1983–84 playoffs, the Oilers were an explosive team that was ready to reel in their first Stanley Cup. The Oilers had been stopped the year before by the four-time champion New York Islanders, but this time they were ready to knock out the champions.

As much as they were fueled by Gretzky and high-scoring defenseman Paul Coffey, it was Kurri's sharpshooting ways that helped propel the Oilers to the title. He was on fire throughout the playoffs as he scored a league-high 14 goals and 14 assists in 19 games. The Oilers and Islanders split the first two games in New York, but once the series got back to Edmonton, the home team flexed their muscles. Edmonton won the series in five games.

Kurri's overpowering playoff performance became commonplace for his team. He scored 19 goals in 18 postseason games during the 1984–85 season. The Oilers swept the Kings and Winnipeg Jets in the first two rounds before beating the Chicago Blackhawks in six games and then taking apart the Philadelphia Flyers the following year.

The Oilers appeared to be at their peak, but they were beaten in the division finals on a fluke "own" goal against the Calgary Flames. Nevertheless, they came back roaring in the 1986–87 season. They finished with the league's best regular-season record, and then rolled to their third title in four seasons.

Kurri was once again the Oilers' go-to man when it came to playoff scoring. He had a league-best 15 goals and 10 assists, and his ability to pick the corners and get his shot away in an instant was no longer seen as anything but a given. No, he did not carry the Oilers on his shoulders—that was still Gretzky's job—but he was the ideal hammer who was able to score at the most important moments of crucial playoff games.

The Oilers won their fourth Stanley Cup the following year, and that was Gretzky's last season with the team. The Oilers took apart the Boston Bruins in four games, and Kurri continued to set standards for playoff scoring. He had 14 postseason goals, once again leading all shooters.

Kurri had four consecutive 50-goal seasons between 1984 and 1987, including a 71-goal season in 1984–85. Kurri was clever around the net and could jump on rebounds and score on deflections, but it was his ability to handle quick passes and get rid of his shot in one quick motion that became Kurri's signature. He became known as the master of the one-timer.

The Gretzky-Kurri partnership was perhaps the best one-two punch in NHL history. It was certainly the most prolific, as Kurri assisted on 196 Gretzky goals. Gretzky certainly paid Kurri back in spades, as he assisted on 364 goals by the right wing.

Kurri stayed with the Oilers for two more years, and he played a key role in the team's fifth Stanley Cup championship following the 1989–90 season when he scored 10 goals and 15 assists, but he ended up in Los Angeles for the 1991–92 season after he was involved in a three-way trade involving the Kings, Oilers, and Flyers.

Kurri was able to continue his partnership with Gretzky once again, and while the Kings did not win the Stanley Cup, they were able to get to the Final in 1993 where the team met the Montreal Canadiens. Kurri was up to his old playoff tricks in that run, scoring nine goals and adding eight assists.

Kurri emphasized what a thrill it was to be a part of that Kings team that helped raise the sport's profile in Southern California. "It was great to be a part of five championship teams with the Oilers," he said. "But that was one of the most exciting runs as well. To play with Wayne in Los Angeles, I was so happy to be a part of that."

#34

Bernie Parent

Two seasons with Boston Bruins. Ten seasons with Philadelphia Flyers. Two season with Toronto Maple Leafs. One season with Philadelphia Blazers (WHA).

Bernie Parent was a goaltending legend who led the Philadelphia Flyers to back–to–back–Stanley Cups in 1974 and '75.

However, prior to his great run with the Flyers, Parent had done little to distinguish himself during his tenure with the Boston Bruins and the Toronto Maple Leafs. Both of those teams had seen his athleticism, quickness, and flashy glove hand, but Parent had struggled

Career regular season:

NHL Career: 608 games, 271-198-121, 2.55 goals–against average, 54 shutouts

Two-time Vezina Trophy winner (Top Goaltender)

Two-time Conn Smythe Trophy winner (Playoffs MVP)

Two-time first-team NHL All-Star

Two-time Stanley Cup winner

Elected to Hall of Fame in 1984

to put it all together until he rejoined the Flyers for his second stint with them in 1972–73.

In many ways, Parent was to goaltending what Sandy Koufax was to pitching. During his early years with the Brooklyn and Los Angeles Dodgers, Koufax struggled with his control and overall effectiveness. It took a spring training adjustment to his mindset (command was more important than velocity) to become baseball's most dominant pitcher.

It was something like that for Parent, although it was more of a change in his comfort level that helped him reach his peak as a goaltender.

Parent grew up in Montreal where hockey is like religion, and his exposure to the game and the Canadiens helped make him a huge fan of goaltender Jacques Plante. He admired everything about the Habs' spectacular goaltender, and he did everything he could to model his game after him.

He got his first chance with the Bruins, who were enamored with his quickness and decisiveness as a junior goalie and minor leaguer. However, when he was brought up to the NHL, he simply performed poorly. Some of that was due to anxiety, and another portion was due to the lack of support he received from a struggling team.

The Bruins gave him a couple of opportunities to show off his ability in the 1965–66 and 1966–67 seasons, and it simply didn't work. They made him available in the expansion draft of '67, and the Flyers selected him.

Parent was happy playing with the expansion team, and while he was not playing with a very talented team, he performed quite well.

Bernie Parent

He had a 2.48 goals-against average for the expansion team and he followed that up with a 2.69 GAA the following year.

There was little reason to think that Parent would be traded at any time in the foreseeable future, but the Flyers had another strong goaltender in Doug Favell. They came to the conclusion that Favell would eventually become their No. 1 goaltender and that Parent would be a better trade asset because he would bring more talent in return than Favell brought at that point.

The Flyers moved Parent to the Maple Leafs in 1971 in a controversial deal that saw them acquire mediocre goalie Bruce Gamble and third-line center Mike "Shakey" Walton. While Favell was a decent goaltender, he was not a game-changing one like Parent would prove to be.

Parent was not happy about the trade because he loved living and playing in Philadelphia. He was solid with Toronto, but a strange incident in the 1971 playoffs was among the more noteworthy aspects of his stay with the Maple Leafs.

Toronto met the Rangers in the playoffs, and the two teams engaged in a bench-clearing brawl in Game 2 at Madison Square Garden. The Leafs were winning and about to square the series and the Rangers were angry and embarrassed since they had the better record and appeared to be the better team. Vic Hadfield of the Rangers grabbed hold of Parent's mask and pulled it off of his head and fired it into the crowd.

In those days, goaltenders had one mask and almost never had replacements for that vital piece of equipment. The Rangers fans had no inclination to return the mask, and Parent could not play without it. Toronto head coach John McLellan pushed Parent to play without it, but he took himself out of the game.

After the 1971–72 season, the World Hockey Association emerged as a competitor to the NHL. Players who felt locked in by the NHL and limited by their contracts had the ability to sign with teams in the competing league for more money.

Parent was one of those and he signed with a team called the Miami Screaming Eagles. Despite that colorful nickname, the

Florida-based team never got off the ground, and he ended up back in Philadelphia—but not with the Flyers. He played for the WHA's Blazers, and that team was a disaster from the start.

After an awful 1972 season with the Blazers, Parent was a free agent and he re-signed with the Flyers. Not only was he relieved and happy to be back in an environment that was favorable for him, but also the Flyers were becoming a powerful team that would soon be a championship contender.

Bringing Parent back was the move the team needed to get to that level. With stars like Bobby Clarke, Rick MacLeish, and Moose Dupont leading the way, the Flyers were a dangerous and aggressive team that was developing a nasty and winning reputation around the league.

Parent gave them championship-level goaltending, and the team was able to fulfill its vast potential in the 1973–74 season. After a dominating regular season, the Flyers swept the Atlanta Flames 4-0 in the first round of the playoffs.

That earned them a spot in the semifinals against the New York Rangers. Up to that point, no expansion team had ever beaten an established Original Six team, but the Flyers were of a mind to change that.

Both teams won their home games through the first six of the series, but most expected the veteran Rangers to prevail in the seventh game in Philadelphia. However, the Flyers pounded the Rangers physically, Parent outplayed excellent Rangers goalie Eddie Giacomin, and the Flyers survived the series.

If the Rangers were a major test, the Flyers and Parent faced the Bruins in their final exam for the Stanley Cup Final. The Bruins had dominated the Flyers for years, and had gone 27 consecutive games without losing to them until the 1973–74 season. The Bruins had Bobby Orr and Phil Esposito and a cast of stars, and it seemed that they would roll to the championship.

The Flyers played the Bruins tough in Game 1 before losing on a late goal by Orr. However, Clarke scored in overtime in Game 2 to give the Flyers the win in Boston they needed if they were going to win the championship.

Parent was at his best in leading the Flyers to wins in all three games played in Philadelphia. The last was a 1-0 victory in Game 6 that featured an array of brilliant saves.

It was clearly the most important game of his career. He made a remarkable save on Ken Hodge's slapshot to the far corner late in the third period and the Spectrum exploded as the Flyers finished off the win.

"It was just remarkable to win the Cup, and to share that with our fans was simply amazing," Parent said. "It was sheer joy for all of us."

The Flyers went on to win the Stanley Cup again the following year as they beat the high-scoring Buffalo Sabres in six games and Parent was once again spectacular.

Parent won the Vezina and Conn Smythe trophies in 1974 and '75. No other goalie has ever pulled off that double.

He remained an outstanding goaltender for the next four years, but an eye injury in 1979 would force him into retirement. Parent was hit by an errant high stick, and his depth perception was permanently damaged as a result of the freakish blow.

That was it for Parent, but he had a remarkable run when he was at his peak, and few goaltenders have ever been able to shut down opponents the way Parent could.

#35

Brian Leetch

Seventeen seasons with New York Rangers. One season with Toronto Maple Leafs. One season with Boston Bruins.

Playing in the National Hockey League was a far-fetched dream for Brian Leetch as a youngster.

Ultimately the first NHL player to have been born in Texas, Leetch learned to skate and play the game at an outdoor public rink in Connecticut. While he was athletic and skilled at a fairly young age, the thought of playing professionally never crossed his mind. However, as Leetch made progress in his career and advanced up the ladder, the idea of playing in the NHL soon became a possibility. He played prep school hockey at Avon Old Farms School, and after scoring 70 goals and 90 assists in 54 games while playing on the blue line, he started to attract attention.

Leetch excelled at every stop, and he began to realize he might have a future in professional hockey. That notion became reality when the New York Rangers drafted him with the ninth pick in the first round of the 1986 draft.

Career regular season:
NHL Career: 1,245 games, 247 goals, 781 assists, 1,028 points.
One-time Calder Trophy winner (Rookie of the Year)
Two-time Norris Trophy winner (Best Defenseman)
One-time Conn Smythe Trophy winner (Playoff MVP)
Three-time first-team NHL All-Star; three-time second-team NHL All-Star
One-time Stanley Cup winner
Elected to Hall of Fame in 2009
Advanced stats: 86.2 OPS, 60.4 DPS, 146.6 PS

Before he signed a contract and played with the Broadway Blueshirts, Leetch played a year of hockey at Boston College and represented the United States in the 1988 Olympics in Calgary.

After the Olympics was over, he was ready to take the plunge. He knew he had been a solid prospect worthy of a pick in the draft, but not every first-round pick turns into a competent NHL player.

Leetch played 17 games towards the end of the 1987–88 season, and that's not enough time to prove anything. However he gave an excellent indication that he belonged in the NHL and that he would be able to make a consistent contribution, as he scored 14 points in those 17 games.

Leetch became a star in the 1988–89 season. He was an outstanding skater with excellent vision of the ice, which are both requirements for playing defense in the NHL. Additionally, he was a very accurate passer, an outstanding stickhandler, and he had a blistering shot from the point.

The Rangers recognized this and he quickly became one of their top defensemen. Leetch scored 23 goals and 71 points in his rookie season, and he won the Calder Trophy as the rookie of the year. He also received votes for the Norris Trophy and the All-Star team.

Leetch joined the Rangers at the same time they were starting to build an impressive team. In addition to Leetch, they built a solid core with Mike Richter in goal, Mark Messier, Adam Graves, and speedster Mike Gartner.

The Rangers had not won a Stanley Cup since 1940, but they were building a powerful club in the early 1990s that certainly had championship dreams within their reach.

After Leetch's powerful rookie year, he continued to improve. The Rangers finished first in the Patrick Division in 1991–92 with 105 points, a figure that was good enough to earn them the President's Trophy.

Leetch had a remarkable season, registering 22 goals and 80 assists, and becoming the first American-born NHL defenseman to exceed the 100-point barrier. That was good enough to earn him the Norris Trophy.

While the Rangers had dreams of winning the Stanley Cup that year, they were stopped short in the second round when they were defeated by the Pittsburgh Penguins.

The Rangers had not displayed the composure needed to win in the playoffs, but Leetch was bound and determined to get there the next season.

"We had an excellent team that season and we were expecting quite a bit from ourselves," Leetch said. "It hurt to lose to the Penguins and after we got over the disappointment, we had to figure out where we were short. It took a little more commitment from everyone on the team, but we knew we were going to get there."

Injuries limited Leetch to 36 games the following season, but he was at full speed and ready to go in 1993–94. The Rangers were brilliant that year, notching a 52-24-8 record and winning the President's Trophy once again with 112 points.

They were determined not to get upended in the early rounds, and with Leetch, Messier, and Richter leading the way, they cruised through the first two rounds of the playoffs in matchups with the New York Islanders and Washington Capitals.

They were tested in a severe manner by the New Jersey Devils in the Eastern Conference Final, and it appeared they were going to face another heartbreaking defeat after they trailed 3-2 following a home loss in the fifth game.

However, they rebounded with a huge victory in Game 6 on the road thanks to heroics from Messier, and they survived a double overtime effort in Game 7 to get to the Stanley Cup Final against the Vancouver Canucks.

Leetch was not about to let this opportunity slip through his grasp. He had been playing exceptional hockey throughout the playoffs, and he was at his best in the final series. He scored four goals and six assists in the first six games against the Canucks, and the two teams were tied at three games each. Leetch was on top of his game in the finale, and he scored a goal as the Rangers pulled out a 3-2 victory and their long-awaited Stanley Cup.

The Rangers had a slew of heroes on that team, and the Conn Smythe Trophy could have gone to Messier, Richter, or Graves, but Leetch had been the most dominant player throughout the Stanley Cup Final and he was voted the award. He became the first American-born player to take home the Conn Smythe Trophy.

The Rangers remained an impressive team, but that was their only Stanley Cup. Leetch continued to play at a very high level as he won the Norris Trophy again following the 1996–97 season in which he had 20 goals and 58 assists.

Leetch stayed with the Rangers until late in the 2003–04 season when the Toronto Maple Leafs picked him up as a late-season acquisition. After the 2004–05 season was wiped out by the NHL's lockout, Leetch finished his career with the Boston Bruins in 2005–06.

Leetch will forever be known as a New York Ranger, but that doesn't quite do him justice. He was inducted into the Hall of Fame in 2009, and he was presented by Messier.

Messier looked over at Leetch as he was introducing him, and he referred to his former teammate and called him the "greatest Ranger of all-time."

Not bad for a Connecticut kid who never even dreamed of playing in the NHL.

#36

Tony Esposito

Fifteen seasons with Chicago Blackhawks. One season with Montreal Canadiens.

W aiting, waiting, and more waiting was the watchword for Tony Esposito before he finally got a legitimate chance to show what kind of goalie he could become at the National Hockey League level. However, once that opportunity came, Esposito proved to be one of the best and most innovative goalies in the history of the sport.

Esposito had played college hockey at Michigan Tech before playing minor-league hockey with the Vancouver Canucks of the

Career regular season:

NHL Career: 886 games, 423-306-151, 2.92 goals-against average, 76 shutouts

Three-time Vezina Trophy winner (Top Goaltender)

One-time Calder Trophy winner (Rookie of the Year)

Three-time first-team NHL All-Star; two-time second-team NHL All-Star

Elected to Hall of Fame in 1988

Western Hockey League (before the team became an NHL franchise). After his stint in Western Canada, he moved to Houston of the Central Hockey League.

He got his first chance to play in the NHL during the 1968–69 season with the Montreal Canadiens. It was not a true chance, because he only played in 13 games. The Canadiens had two established goalies at the time in Rogatien Vachon and Gump Worsley, so Esposito never figured into the big picture.

But the Chicago Blackhawks had kept their eyes on Esposito throughout the years, and they jumped on the chance to acquire him when the Habs made him available in the intraleague draft.

Head coach Billy Reay thought he was getting a competent goalie who could help the Hawks make the playoffs. However, he got much more than that.

Esposito proved to be a record-setting goalie who helped Chicago secure first place in the NHL's powerful East Division.

It was a remarkable year for both Esposito and the Blackhawks. Esposito was just another unknown hopeful at the start of the season, but by the time the 1969–70 season was over, he had recorded a league-best 15 shutouts. Nevertheless, Esposito tried to deflect the credit from himself to his teammates for the plethora of shutouts.

"It really was a team effort that season," Esposito recalled. "You won't find a better indication of how hard the guys played in front of me than from the number of shutouts that we had. It was all about strong positional play by our defensemen and forwards and just a tremendous amount of desire. If we were blanking a team going into the third period, guys would talk to each other about getting that

Tony Esposito

shutout. It mattered to everybody. I just happened to be the goalie who was playing with those guys and I couldn't have been happier to be working with such a great bunch of guys."

While the shutout numbers were eye-catching, Esposito also had a 38-17-8 record that season along with a 2.17 goals-against average. He gave the Blackhawks anywhere from steady to spectacular play at a position they had been struggling at for several seasons.

Esposito changed the way goalies played the game. Before he took over in the Blackhawks' net, nearly all goaltenders played the stand-up style and would kick out with their right or left leg when shots went to either corner of the net. Goaltenders were hesitant to go down on the ice to make saves because they feared it would put them out of position for rebounds or quick goalmouth passes.

Esposito didn't hesitate to go down on the ice with his inverted butterfly style. His normal pose was to leave the 5-hole wide open and serve as an inviting target for shooters. Esposito was betting that he could crash down on his pads and close that hole before shooters could expose that opening.

Esposito was quite successful at taking that spot away from shooters. However, most observers felt he was vulnerable on high shots and that he could be beaten regularly to the upper half of the net. "Tony O" negated that perceived weakness with one of the quickest glove hands in the league. He had superb reactions and was capable of stopping most high shots—as long as he was not screened.

The Blackhawks were beaten in the semifinal round of the 1970 Stanley Cup playoffs by the Boston Bruins, the team they had battled for the top spot in the regular season. While the Blackhawks earned first place because they had more victories than Boston, they were swept in four straight games. What made it perhaps even more painful for Esposito is that his brother Phil was virtually unstoppable during that series.

Phil Esposito camped out in the slot and Bobby Orr got him the puck on a regular basis. Phil beat his younger brother with an array of snap shots, wrist shots, and backhanders. It seemed that every loose puck found its way onto Phil's stick and he did not miss.

The following season, the Blackhawks beat the Philadelphia Flyers in four straight games before meeting a razor-sharp New York Rangers team in the semifinals. With both teams playing superb hockey, the Blackhawks survived the series in seven games and Esposito's excellent goaltending helped give him and his team a narrow victory over counterpart Eddie Giacomin and the Rangers.

That gave the Blackhawks a chance to play the Montreal Canadiens in the Stanley Cup Final. That series also went seven games, and the Blackhawks appeared to have the edge as they grabbed a 2-0 lead in the second period before the raucous fans at the Chicago Stadium. However, the game turned when Jacques Lemaire of the Canadiens ripped a shot from just past center ice beyond Esposito's normally reliable glove.

The Habs eventually tied the score and then won the game on a brilliant goal by Henri Richard.

Esposito and the Blackhawks would be haunted by that near-miss for decades. Chicago got back to the Stanley Cup Final against Montreal two years later, and they lost that series in six games.

Esposito's career was marked by it consistency. He was a first- or second-team All-Star five times and he won the Vezina Trophy three times. Additionally, the Blackhawks made the playoffs every year of his career, and while he never played on a Stanley Cup-winning team, his unique style and superb glove hand made him one of the most difficult goaltenders to beat.

#37

Billy Smith

Seventeen seasons with New York Islanders. One season with Los Angeles Kings.

There was nothing laid back or routine about the way Billy Smith played hockey. He was not known as a technician or for his great glove hand.

He was known for his ability to win clutch games and his nasty, vicious play when anyone came near his crease.

Career regular season:

NHL Career: 680 games, 305-233-105, 3.17 goals-against average, 22 shutouts

One-time Vezina Trophy winner (Top Goaltender)

One-time Conn Smythe Trophy winner (Playoffs MVP)

One-time William Jennings Trophy winner (Fewest Goals Scored Against)

One-time first-team NHL All-Star

Four-time Stanley Cup winner

Elected to Hall of Fame in 1993

Smith played in a high-scoring era and he was one of the main reasons the New York Islanders reeled off four straight Stanley Cups between 1980 and '83. His rise to the top was anything but smooth, and if he had not been such a determined and self-confident man, he could have had his career hamstrung on a number of occasions.

Smith was drafted by the Los Angeles Kings in the fifth round of the 1970 draft. The Kings had a strong goaltender in Rogie Vachon, though. When they made Smith available in the 1972 expansion draft, the Islanders snagged him.

That was good news and bad news, because he got a chance to play regularly for the expansion team, but they were just woeful in their early years.

A look at Smith's numbers in the expansion season of 1972–73 shows that he had a 7-24-3 record with a 4.16 goals-against average. However, Smith's performance brings up Tom Hanks's criticism of the women's baseball team he managed in the movie *A League of Their Own*. As Hanks critiques his team, he asks coach Robert Wuhl about his team's record. "We're 8 and 24," Wuhl reports.

"How'd we ever win eight? It's a miracle."

That's the same kind of team that the Islanders had that first year and they weren't much better the following year. But even though the Islanders' defense was slow, inefficient, and didn't play a physical game, Smith played hard every night. He set an example that the other players on the team could follow when it came to effort and playing in a professional manner.

Billy Smith

The Islanders wouldn't remain down in the dumps for long, as general manager Bill Torrey upgraded the team every year and head coach Al Arbour got the best out of his players.

"You have to give [general manager] Bill Torrey a lot of credit," Smith admits. "He got young guys—Denis [Potvin] and Boss [Mike Bossy] and [Clark] Gillies. He was willing to wait. The young guys coming up went through growing pains. Torrey and [coach Al] Arbour were patient with the guys."

Smith established himself as the team's No. 1 goalie, and the Islanders improved enough to make the playoffs in the 1974–75 season.

The team went on a remarkable playoff run in the spring of '75, as they showed none of the nervousness that inexperienced teams are expected to have. They beat the established Rangers in the preliminary round, and that shocking victory gave the Islanders confidence as they moved on to the second round against the Pittsburgh Penguins.

They dropped the first three games against the Pens, but they roared back to take the next four and become the second team in NHL history to overcome an 0–3 deficit and win a playoff series. If that wasn't enough, they fell behind the defending Stanley Cup champion Philadelphia Flyers in the next round by the same margin and then came back to tie the series before falling in the seventh game.

The Islanders got tremendous goaltending in the playoffs, but it came from rookie Chico Resch, and not Smith. Resch just happened to have the hot hand, and Arbour rode him as far as he could.

That could have shaken Smith badly and made him think that his coach and his teammates lost confidence in him. Instead, it just made Smith more determined. While Arbour would go on to say that the Islanders "had two No. 1 goalies" for the next few years, it was Smith who got the opportunity to play in most of the team's playoff games.

Resch was a good goalie and he was the perfect complement for Smith, but Battling Billy gave the Islanders a chance to win every night. He did not look like a great athlete, but he was surprisingly agile and always one of the most competitive players on the ice.

He was very protective of his crease. Opponents who tried to camp out in front of him with the hope of deflecting a shot, jumping on a rebound, or just screening Smith were met with his dominating goalie stick.

Smith would not hesitate to come down on the shins, ankles, and feet of opponents who tried to obscure his vision. He was one of the toughest goalies to ever play the game, and unlike most netminders, he would not hesitate to throw off his catching glove and his blocker and start fighting.

Smith's fire and consistency gave the Islanders a chance to win every night. He backstopped the team to its first championship in 1980, and when Bob Nystrom scored an overtime goal in Game 6 of the Stanley Cup Final against the Philadelphia Flyers, a dynasty was born.

"I think we lost a couple of Stanley Cups before we won the first one because we just didn't know what it took," Smith said. "We caught a couple of teams sleeping right at the beginning and then in the end against Philly, we scored in overtime in the sixth. I'll predict today that if we had lost that game on Long Island we would have our hands more than full in Philadelphia. We would have been pretty shaken. But we had a good team, we had a good system, and we stuck with it even in overtime and we got a break at the right time."

Smith was not known for his scintillating goals-against average during his career; he allowed 3.17 goals per game. However, during the prime of his career, his GAA was below 3.00 in eight of nine seasons.

But what made Smith so tough was the way he played when the Islanders were tied or ahead by a goal in the third period. When the game was on the line, he would simply not get beaten.

#38

Bob Gainey

Sixteen seasons with Montreal Canadiens.

What was Sam Pollock thinking when he selected Bob Gainey with the Montreal Canadiens' No. 1 pick in the 1973 draft?

Gainey had been an impressive junior player with the Peterborough Petes of the Ontario Hockey League because of his brilliant skating speed and his impressive defensive play, but Gainey was not a sniper. He often broke into the open and had many chances to score, but he simply did not have the release that would allow him to become a top scorer in the NHL.

Career regular season:

1,160 games, 239 goals, 262 assists, 501 points

One-time Conn Smythe Trophy winner (Playoff MVP)

Four-time Frank Selke Trophy winner (Best Defensive Forward)

Five Stanley Cup championships

Advanced stats: 8.8 OPS, 18.0 DPS, 26.8 PS

Elected to Hall of Fame in 1992

Good, solid, functional team player? Yes. Superstar worthy of a first-round pick? No way.

At least that was the thought process of most of the hockey world. Pollock had been the architect of Montreal's rise, but few thought he knew what he was doing with the selection of Gainey.

That was more than OK with Pollock. He was not doing his job to win public approval. The only thing he wanted was to bring the Habs championships, and he wanted lots of them.

Pollock, of course, turned out to have the last laugh. The Canadiens would surge in the NHL and join previous Montreal teams as revered Stanley Cup champions. The Canadiens won the sport's top honor in the spring of 1976, and would defend that title the following three years as well.

While Guy Lafleur, Jacques Lemaire, Steve Shutt, Larry Robinson, Guy Lapointe, Serge Savard, and Ken Dryden were all key parts of what probably was the best and most dominant dynasty in the history of the sport, Gainey also played a huge role and may have been the backbone of this elite team.

You would never know it by merely looking at his statistics. Gainey never scored more than 23 goals in any of his sixteen seasons with the Canadiens, but he was one of the best players on the team by his second year.

Gainey played 66 games as a rookie in 1973-74, and while it may have looked like he was overmatched after scoring three goals and seven assists, he was merely learning the ropes. He put it together in 1974–75 and tallied 17 goals and 20 assists, but those numbers had little to do with the way Gainey was contributing. He was already a

Bob Gainey

superior defensive player capable of shutting down the opponents' best skaters and scorers.

He was also a fearsome body checker who would pick up steam as the game went along. If Gainey was a hard-edged tough guy in the first period, he was a wrecking crew if the game was still on the line in the third period. If the Canadiens were protecting a one-goal lead in the final 20 minutes, head coach Scotty Bowman was as comfortable putting out his second-year defensive stalwart as he was with the explosive scoring of Lafleur. Each player could ensure a victory, even though they did it in completely different styles.

The Canadiens' Stanley Cup in 1976 came against the two-time defending champion Philadelphia Flyers. Many around the league were openly rooting for the swift-skating Habs to unseat the Broad Street Bullies, who were known more for brawling and mayhem than they were for skill. Gainey and Robinson played a huge role in bullying the bullies as the talented Canadiens registered a four-game sweep.

The victory was a seminal moment for Gainey, who got to bask in the glow of championship glory.

"The first time that you actually get through that doorway and walk into the winner's circle is a time that all players will remember because it's a goal that all players have," said Gainey. "Until you've reached that goal, then it's always out in front of you. When you have that opportunity, the moment is one that leaves a mark on your trip through life and trip through your career."

Gainey was absolutely relentless when he skated, and never took a shift off. He was so good at his job that he was the main reason the NHL created the Frank Selke Trophy that goes to the NHL's best defensive forward. The league first presented the trophy following the 1977–78 season, and Gainey was the runaway winner. He also happened to win it the next three seasons as well.

What Bobby Orr was to defensemen, Gainey was to defensive forwards. During his era with the Canadiens, he had a certain flair to his defensive game. Not only would he play a physical game against forwards who liked to skate and make plays in the open ice, but he anticipated what they would do next and beat them to the spot.

This allowed him to intercept passes and ruin scoring opportunities.

Gainey may not have been a brilliant scorer himself, but he was effective on the offensive end. He scored 20 goals for the first time in the 1978–79 season, and he was the best player the Canadiens had in the playoffs.

He scored six goals and had 10 assists in the Habs' 16 playoff games against the Maple Leafs, Bruins, and Rangers, and Gainey was awarded the Conn Smythe Trophy as the postseason MVP.

Gainey was named captain of the Canadiens following the retirement of Savard, and he was the link that the young Canadiens had to the glory years of the 1970s. While he had not played with Jean Beliveau, he did have the opportunity to play with Yvan Cournoyer.

He knew the team's tradition like the back of his own hand, and he was the perfect role player for what may have been the best team in the sport's history. Gainey may not have been a coach or general manager at the time, but it was clear that he was on that path because he was serious in the way he played, practiced, and carried out his duties as captain.

The Canadiens would win one more Stanley Cup with Gainey wearing the captain's "C," and that would come in 1986.

Unlike the dynastic champions of the late 1970s who rolled to their glory as overwhelming favorites, the '86 Canadiens were underdogs who finished second in the Adams Division to the Quebec Nordiques.

Few expected Montreal to get past the second round. However, with rookie Patrick Roy in the net, they rolled past the Bruins in the first round and then needed overtime of the seventh game to get by the Hartford Whalers in the second round.

They dispatched the Rangers in five games to win the Eastern Conference and then outlasted Calgary in six games to win their twenty-third Stanley Cup.

Gainey was still a relentless player at that point in his career, and he also had five goals and five assists in 20 playoff games. As captain, he became the first player to lift the Cup after the great championship trophy was awarded.

Bob Gainey

It was a fitting honor for a player who may be the greatest defensive forward in the history of the game. Nothing against Mr. Selke, but renaming that trophy for Bob Gainey would be one of the best things the NHL could do to honor this unsung superstar.

Oh, and by the way, Sam Pollock clearly knew what he was doing when he selected Gainey.

#39

Mike Gartner

Ten seasons with Washington Capitals. Five seasons with New York Rangers. Three seasons with Toronto Maple Leafs. Two seasons with Minnesota North Stars. Two seasons with Phoenix Coyotes. One season with Cincinnati Stingers (WHA).

If you wanted a player who could provide instant offense, Mike Gartner was one of the best at his craft. Gartner had explosive speed and when he turned on the jets, he created scoring opportunities for himself and his teammates. Gartner and Wayne Gretzky both entered the NHL in the 1979–80 season, and that's because

Mike Gartner

both players had been in the World Hockey Association the year before. The 1978–79 season was the last year that the WHA competed. Since the Edmonton Oilers was one of four teams absorbed by the NHL— the Quebec Nordiques,

> **Career regular season:**
> NHL Career: 1,432 games, 708 goals, 627 assists, 1,335 points.
> WHA: 78 games, 27 goals, 25 assists, 52 points
> Elected to Hall of Fame in 2001
> **Advanced stats: 100.1 OPS, 21.7 DPS, 121.8 PS**

Winnipeg Jets and Hartford Whalers were the others—they got to keep Gretzky on their roster.

However, the Cincinnati Stingers were not retained, and since Gartner had played one year with that team and had been an underage player by the NHL's standards, he went into the NHL amateur draft. The Washington Capitals selected fourth in 1979, and they picked the explosive Gartner.

Gartner is like the rest of the hockey world in that he looks up to Gretzky's tremendous level of success and accomplishment. However, there's one area where Gartner has Gretzky beaten—as well as nearly every other player who has ever competed in the NHL— flat-out speed.

If you wanted a player to skate from one end of the ice to the other in a dead sprint, you would not find someone who could beat Gartner. He also had quick moves that allowed him to get free in the offensive zone, but it was his ability to get from Point A to Point B that really made him a special and memorable player throughout his career.

Gartner's speed was an important factor in his ability to play consistently throughout his twenty years. He was able to skate away from trouble, avoid big hits from bigger and nastier players and put his wicked shot on net.

Gartner had shown what he could do at the professional level in his lone season in Cincinnati, as he scored 27 goals and 25 assists in the WHA, which was a high-quality league throughout the majority of its run. While the overall play in that league may have slipped a bit in that last season, Gartner developed the confidence to know that he could score against experienced professionals.

"The WHA was a very good league; probably not as good as the NHL but just a small step down," Gartner said. "It was a great experience for an eighteen-year-old kid to get a chance to play hockey and be away from home and start the dream. The next year, the WHA merged with the NHL and it was a new beginning."

He needed very little adjustment time to make an impact in the NHL. Gartner gave the Capitals a dose of instant offense as he scored 36 goals and 32 assists as a twenty-year-old rookie. While those numbers would be worthy of Calder Trophy status in many years, Gartner was beaten out by Bobby Smith of the Minnesota North Stars, who tallied 30 goals and 44 assists.

Gartner was a consistent scorer throughout his run with the Capitals. He scored 40 goals or more five times in his nine full seasons with the Capitals and he never scored fewer than 35 goals in any of those seasons. When he scored 48 goals in his second full season in Washington as a twenty-one-year-old player, he established himself as one of the most dangerous players in the league.

While Gartner was becoming one of the league's most consistent scorers, he was helping to make the Caps a very difficult team to play against. Washington had been an expansion team in 1974–75, and they had been relatively unsuccessful through the 1979–80 season. However, they became much more competitive in 1980–81 and they would make the playoffs for the first time in the 1982–83 season. Much of that was due to Gartner's high-scoring ways.

Gartner's speed was a game-planning factor for opposing coaches. If teams were going to beat the Caps, they had to find a way to stop or at least slow down Gartner by making it difficult for him to take possession of the puck at full speed. Since he also had the quickness to get away from checkers, that assignment was quite difficult to accomplish.

Mike Gartner

The Caps became a consistent playoff team, but they rarely had success once they reached the postseason. They failed to make noise in the postseason until 1987–88, when they beat the Philadelphia Flyers in seven games and that allowed them to engage the New Jersey Devils in the second round. That was another seven-game series, and the Caps dropped that series when they couldn't secure a final-game victory at home.

If there was ever a knock on Gartner's play, it was probably his inability to play as well in the postseason as he had in the regular season. Through the 1990–91 season, Gartner never scored more than five goals in any playoff year.

That would finally change in the 1991–92 season when Gartner was playing for the New York Rangers. He scored eight goals and eight assists in 13 games for the Blueshirts, and for once had that magic touch in the playoffs that had eluded him throughout the majority of his career.

Gartner had never come close to winning the Stanley Cup in his career, but it appeared he might have a chance in 1993–94, as the Rangers were having a dream season. However, he was traded to the Toronto Maple Leafs prior to the trade deadline for Glenn Anderson, and Gartner had to watch the Rangers win their first Stanley Cup in fifty-four years.

At the time, the Maple Leafs were situated in the Western Conference, and they went on an excellent playoff run of their own. They beat the Chicago Blackhawks and San Jose Sharks in the first two rounds before losing to the Vancouver Canucks in the Western Conference Final. Gartner had five goals and six assists in Toronto's postseason run.

Gartner does not have a championship or any major awards on his resume, but he scored 30 goals or more in fifteen consecutive seasons. The only thing that stopped that streak was the lockout-shortened 1994–95 season, and Gartner bounced back and scored 35 goals in 1995–96 and 32 in 1996–97. He retired after the 1997–98 season.

Few players have ever been as consistent as Gartner in terms of effort and production. "I tried to show up to play every night and tried to contribute to the team," Gartner said. "I was able to stay relatively healthy, and that was a big factor for me."

It was a brilliant and memorable career, and Gartner was elected to the Hall of Fame in 2001.

#40

Alex Ovechkin (through 2014–15)

Ten seasons with Washington Capitals.

If you like your hockey players shy, humble, and self-effacing, Alex Ovechkin is not your man.

While many hockey players have those type of low-key personality traits and love to talk about what's good for the team and hate to talk about personal achievements, Ovechkin is not one of those types.

From the moment he was selected with the No. 1 pick in the 2004 draft by the Washington Capitals, Ovechkin has wanted to do one thing—put the puck in the net and keep doing it until he

Career regular season:

NHL Career: 760 games, 475 goals, 420 assists, 895 points

One-time Art Ross winner (Leading Scorer)

Two-time Hart Trophy winner (MVP)

Three-time Ted Lindsay Award winner (Most Outstanding Player)

Four-time Maurice Richard Trophy winner (Leading Goal Scorer)

Four-time first-team NHL All-Star; one-time second-team NHL All-Star

One-time Maurice Richard Trophy winner (Leading Goal Scorer)

One-time Calder Trophy winner (Rookie of the Year)

Six-time first-team NHL All-Star, three-time second-team NHL All-Star

Advanced stats: 103.1 OPS, 18.0 DPS, 121.1 PS

was recognized as the best player on the planet.

Ovechkin has emphasized the importance of winning and in 2013-14 and 2014–15, it looked like winning had become far more important to him than it had ever been in the past. However, while a championship legacy is important to many players, it has sometimes seemed like a personal legacy is far more important to Ovechkin.

While some have accused Ovechkin of being selfish throughout his run with the Washington Capitals, he is certainly not a liar or a phony.

But he is talented and has a knack for putting the puck in the net, and he also has a huge personality. The Russian dynamo is one of the best goal scorers in league history, and he set the tone in his rookie season.

Ovechkin played one more year with his hometown Dynamo Moscow the season after he was drafted by Washington, but he decided to play in the NHL the next season. Though he was just twenty, it was obvious in training camp that Ovechkin had explosive skating ability, a huge shot, and the kind of strength needed to hold his own in the corners with veteran NHL defensemen. At 6-3 and 230 pounds, Ovechkin excelled at a big man's game.

Alex Ovechkin (through 2014–15)

Ovechkin scored 52 goals and 54 assists as he won the Calder Trophy, became a first-team NHL All-Star, and finished sixth in the MVP voting.

Winning the Calder was a big statement for Ovechkin, because he was up against Sidney Crosby, who had been taken with the No. 1 pick in 2005. The two men quickly built a nasty rivalry that is rarely seen in the sport.

Ovechkin's aggressive personality seemed to rub Crosby the wrong way. He was a shy kid from the Canadian prairies, and he was one of those players who believed in team-first. As a result, the two players were diametrically opposed on a lot of issues, and any game between Ovechkin's Capitals and Crosby's Penguins was worth the price of admission.

Ovechkin quickly became a goal-scoring machine. After his brilliant rookie season, he had a solid second season with 46 goals and 46 assists before turning it on for Years 3 and 4.

Ovechkin was an unstoppable force in the 2007–08 season, as he blasted home 65 goals and 47 assists. In addition to landing first-team All-Star status for the fourth straight season, he won the Ross Trophy as the league's leading scorer and also earned the Hart Trophy as the league's MVP, beating out Crosby, who had won the award the year before.

Ovechkin continued to roll the following year and he scored 56 goals and 54 assists as he won the Hart Trophy for a second consecutive year. Ovechkin scored 50 goals in 2009–10, and that made four years out of his first five in which he had scored 50 or more.

While Ovechkin was piling up his individual accolades, his Capitals were not faring well in the postseason. They lost a first-round series to the Philadelphia Flyers in 2007–08, and the sting of that defeat was made that much worse because Crosby and the Penguins made it all the way to the Stanley Cup Final.

The following year, the Caps won their first-round matchup with the New York Rangers, while the Penguins defeated the Flyers. That set up an epic second-round meeting between Ovechkin and the Capitals and Crosby and his Penguins.

It was a memorable series and when the Caps won Game 6 in Pittsburgh on an overtime goal by David Steckel, the Caps had a chance to close out the series at home before their raucous fans.

Ovechkin may have enjoyed all of his 50-goal seasons, but he did not want to lose to Crosby and the Pens. The Caps were amped up as they took the ice, but the Penguins played like champions and rolled to a decisive 6-2 victory. Pittsburgh opened up a 5-0 lead before Ovechkin scored to get the Caps on the board, but it was too little and too late. Crosby scored two goals and an assist in the decisive victory over his rival.

It hurt that much more later in the spring when the Penguins went on to win the Stanley Cup.

Ovechkin seemed to take that defeat to heart, and he followed that up with a 32-goal season in 2010-11 and 38 the following year.

He also appeared to be out of it for much of the 2012–13 season when half the year was lost due to a lockout. Nevertheless, he suddenly caught fire in the last six weeks and finished as the league's leading goal scorer with 32 goals (in just 48 games).

Ovechkin found his goal-scoring mojo once again in 2013–14 and 2014–15, when he topped the 50-goal mark.

However, there was something missing from the Capitals play in the postseason. They blew a 3-1 lead to the Rangers in the second round of the 2015 playoffs, and they simply lacked the finishing ability to come through in the playoff when they had a chance. The Capitals typically win in the first round, but Ovechkin has never been able to get past the second round in any of his first ten seasons.

Ovechkin may be getting tired of losing. After former Nashville Predators boss Barry Trotz was brought into coach the team prior to the 2014–15 season, Ovechkin seemed to be a much more determined player. Instead of merely playing hard in the offensive zone, Ovechkin used his speed to back check and play defense, and also throw heavy body checks against his opponents.

If he continues to show that same kind of devotion, the Caps may finally advance past the second round.

#41

Darryl Sittler

Twelve seasons with Toronto Maple Leafs. Three seasons with Philadelphia Flyers. One season with Detroit Red Wings.

Darryl Sittler was a phenom when he was coming out of junior hockey.

It's a long way from stardom as a junior player to actually making an NHL roster, but the Toronto Maple Leafs were all but certain when they drafted him in 1970 that Sittler would not only make the team but even become a star. Every scout and executive had seen Sittler play in person and the conclusions were nearly unanimous.

Career regular season:
1,096 games, 484 goals, 637 assists, 1,121 points
One-time second-team NHL All-Star
Advanced stats: 81.0 OPS, 14.8 DPS, 95.8 PS
Elected to Hall of Fame in 1989

There was no doubt that he would be successful, because of his speed, instincts, passing ability, and big shot, but there was a key adjustment that Sittler would have to make. He had played center throughout his junior career and the Leafs felt they had plenty of talent at that position with veterans Dave Keon, Norm Ullman, Mike "Shakey" Walton, and Jim Harrison. They wanted Sittler to play left wing.

There was no pushback from Sittler, who only wanted to make the team in his rookie year. He did enough to win head coach John McLellan's confidence and approval, but the first two years of his career didn't go well for Sittler. In addition to the usual rookie adjustments, he broke his wrist. That kept him from playing his game the way he wanted to. It impacted his stickhandling, passing, and had a significant impact on his ability to shoot the puck.

He wasn't at 100 percent until the start of his third season, which also marked his return to center. Harrison had defected to the World Hockey Association, while Norm Ullman got injured. Sittler hit his stride in the 1972–73 season, scoring 29 goals and registering 48 assists while playing between Rick Kehoe and Dennis Dupere.

That was an important season for Sittler, because his initial contract with the Leafs concluded with that season, and if he wanted to stay with them, he needed to produce. General manager Jim Gregory was impressed with what he saw and he gave Sittler a five-year deal.

The Leafs made an excellent investment. Sittler immediately became one of the game's elite players. He paid off handsomely in 1973–74 by scoring 38 goals and 46 assists, and he showed his consistency the following year by scoring 36 goals and adding 44 assists.

Darryl Sittler

Sittler's on-ice performance along with his leadership in the locker room gave him enhanced credibility throughout the league. The Leafs pinned extra responsibility on him by naming Sittler captain.

It was a role that suited him well, because he was naturally inclined to stick up for his teams and set an example by the way he played.

The 1975–76 season was another excellent year for Sittler, and it saw him shatter the NHL record book one night with a remarkable performance against the Boston Bruins.

On February 7, 1976, Sittler went to Maple Leaf Gardens thinking it would be a long night. The visiting Bruins had won seven games in a row, while the Leafs had won just one of their last seven games.

But there was a glimmer of hope because the Bruins were starting an inexperienced rookie backup goalie named Dave Reece. The first period was fairly uneventful, but the Leafs came out of it with a 2-1 lead and Sittler had assisted on both goals.

That's a fairly good night right there, but the performance turned magical in the second period when Sittler scored three goals and added two more assists. The normally disciplined Bruins were having a rough night defensively, and it seemed that Sittler was there to take advantage every time he stepped on the ice.

When he came out to start the third period, he already had seven points. "I figured that was it for me and I wouldn't do any more scoring," Sittler recalled. "Whoever scores seven points in a game? I didn't think I was going to get any more."

But he did. He scored a power play goal early in the third period on a pass from defenseman Borje Salming, and then converted a pass from Errol Thompson midway through the frame for his fifth goal of the game. Sittler heard the Maple Leaf Gardens announcer tell the crowd that he had just broken the NHL record for points in a game with nine.

"I heard that and the fans gave me a standing ovation," Sittler said. "It sent chills down my spine."

Later in the third period, Sittler had the puck as he was coming out from the corner. He spotted an open teammate standing in front of the net and he quickly fired a pass to him. However, the puck hit

Bruins defenseman Brad Park in the skates and went through Reece for the final goal of the game. Sittler had scored six goals and added four assists for a remarkable 10-point game.

"The noise was just incredible at that point," Sittler said. "Everyone was screaming and my teammates were all over me. No matter whatever happens, I will never forget that night."

As explosive as that game was for Sittler, he had another brilliant night seven months later while playing for Canada in the championship round of the Canada Cup against Czechoslovakia. The Czechs had beaten Team Canada in the round-robin portion of the tournament, while the Canadians had won the first game of the championship round.

The second game of the best-of-three series was very tight and the Canadians sent it to overtime on a late goal by Philadelphia's Bill Barber. Both teams had great chances in the overtime, but Sittler ended matters a little over 11 minutes in when he took a pass from Marcel Dionne and streaked down the left side on Vladimir Dzurilla. Bruins coach Don Cherry had been an assistant for Canada, and he advised the team that Dzurilla went way out of his net to cut down the angle.

He told his players to fake the shot, keep skating, and they would have an open net to shoot at. With that in mind, Sittler faked his big slapshot, took one more stride, and wristed the puck into the net for the Canada Cup winner.

"The surge of pride I felt was indescribable," Sittler said. "To score a goal like that for my country was unbelievable."

The Leafs were not a championship-level team. While Sittler had consistent season after consistent season, his team made it as far as the semifinals one time, and they were swept by the powerful Montreal Canadiens.

He closed his career with three seasons in Philadelphia and one in Detroit, and while his teams made it to the playoffs each of those years, they could never make it out of the first round.

But few players could ever match Sittler's competitiveness, and no player has ever come close to the 10-point night that he had in 1976.

#42

Joe Sakic

Twenty seasons with Quebec Nordiques/Colorado Avalanche.

T ake a look at Joe Sakic's career numbers and achievements and it's clear that he was a very special hockey player throughout the whole of his career with the Quebec Nordiques and the Colorado Avalanche.

He was a spectacular winner with two Stanley Cups, a gold medal in the Olympics, gold in the World Cup of Hockey, gold in the world championships, and gold in the World Junior Championships.

Career regular season:

1,378 games, 625 goals, 1,016 assists, 1,641 points

One-time Conn Smythe Trophy winner (Playoff MVP)

One-time Hart Trophy winner (MVP)

One-time Lady Byng Trophy winner (Gentlemanly Play)

One-time Ted Lindsay Award winner (Outstanding Offensive Player)

Three-time first-team NHL All-Star

Two-time Stanley Cup champion

Advanced stats: 141.7 OPS, 26.1 DPS, 167.8 PS

Elected to Hall of Fame in 2012

At every one of those levels, there was a moment when coaches, teammates and fans knew that if the team was going to come through, Sakic was going to rise to the occasion with a big moment. He almost never failed at the most important moments.

The numbers bear him out. During his twenty-year career in the NHL, Sakic scored 625 goals and 1,016 assists. He averaged 1.19 points per game in his career, and while that is not quite Gretzky- or Lemieux-like, it puts him in elite company with the best players who have ever competed in the game.

Yet numbers and championships don't tell the full story about Sakic. He was a leader in the locker room and he usually did it in quiet fashion. But if he did speak, everyone took notice and would pay heed to his words.

Sakic had already established himself as a full-fledged NHL star by his fourth season in 1991–92. He had broken the 100-point barrier in each of his two previous seasons, and nearly reached the 50-goal mark in 1990–91 when he finished the year with 48 goals.

Despite his achievements, the Nordiques were struggling to win games and they had been dealt a huge blow when No. 1 draft pick Eric Lindros refused to consider signing with the Nordiques and decided to sit out a full season rather than go to French-speaking Quebec City.

Joe Sakic

While most of Sakic's teammates refused to comment publicly about Lindros's refusal to even consider playing for the Nordiques, Sakic spoke bluntly about it.

"We only want players here who have the passion to play the game," Sakic said. "I'm tired of hearing that name. He's not here and there are a lot of others in this lockerroom who really care about the game."

Sakic spoke from the heart and led with his gut, and he had the same characteristics on the ice. He had a remarkable ability to make plays when his team needed them most, and that's why he was such a special player.

While Sakic was playing north of the border during the Nordiques' portion of his career, there was a lot of losing going on throughout the organization. However, when the team moved to Denver and became the Colorado Avalanche prior to the 1995–96 season, the team had turned the corner. Not only would the Avs become a solid contender, but they would also win the first Stanley Cup in their history in the Mile-High City.

The Avs finished with the second-best record in the league during the regular season as they won the Pacific Division with a 47-25-10 mark that was good for 104 points. However, they finished 27 points behind a powerful Detroit Red Wings team that was expected to roll to the Stanley Cup.

Someone forgot to send the memo to the Avalanche and Sakic. Colorado defeated Vancouver in the first round, and followed that up with a victory over Chicago in the second round. Both of those series wins came in six games.

The Avs met the Red Wings in the Western Conference Final, and Colorado played with an edge and confidence even though Detroit appeared to have the advantage. It was Sakic who showed them the way with four goals and six assists as the Avalanche registered the six-game upset. Colorado won the first two games of the series in Detroit, and the Red Wings were never able to climb back in it.

Every time it looked like Detroit might have a chance to get close, it was Sakic who scored a big goal or set up a teammate with a perfect pass.

The Avalanche would roll to their first Stanley Cup by beating an overmatched Florida Panthers team in four games in the Stanley Cup Final.

Sakic had many gifts on the ice including his speed and shockingly powerful and accurate shot, but the two most important factors that set him apart were his ability to anticipate the play and get one step ahead of it and his fearlessness at going into the most competitive areas in front of the net and coming away with the puck.

Teammate Uwe Krupp, who scored the Stanley Cup-winning goal in Game 4 against the Panthers, was amazed by Sakic's ability to make decisive plays in tight spaces.

"He's ordinary Joe until he steps out of a phone booth and it's like he's Super Joe," Krupp told Larry Wigge of NHL.com. "Suddenly he skates away from everyone and he's Michael Jordan, Wayne Gretzky, and John Elway rolled into one, leading the Avalanche up and down the ice. You shake your head and say, 'Where'd he come from?'"

Sakic was at his best in the postseason, and when those games went into overtime, his success was remarkable. Sakic scored eight playoff overtime goals for the Avalanche, and that's more than any other player who has ever competed in the NHL.

Sakic was never interested in the individual accolades that came his way. He wanted the Avalanche to win championships, and he was fairly frustrated after the 1996 title because his team would fall short in the ensuing playoff runs. He wanted another, and it would come five years later.

The Avs had acquired defenseman Ray Bourque from the Boston Bruins who was near the end of his career but desperate to win a Stanley Cup for the first time. While his team would fall short in the 2000 playoffs, the Avs were poised for a long run in 2001.

They were pushed hard throughout the postseason, but they got to the Stanley Cup Final after beating the Canucks (four games), Kings (seven games), and Blues (five games). However, they had their toughest matchup in the Stanley Cup Final against goalie Martin Brodeur and the New Jersey Devils.

Joe Sakic

Sakic and goalie Patrick Roy were motivated to win the title for themselves and Bourque, who would retire at the end of the season. Sakic scored 13 goals and 13 assists in the playoffs that season, and the championship round came down to the seventh game.

Sakic refused to let the Avs lose, scoring a goal and an assist in the decisive game as Colorado pulled out a 3–1 victory.

As captain, Sakic was the first player to handle the Stanley Cup and he skated briefly with it. However, he appeared even more thrilled to hand the trophy to Bourque than he was to skate with it himself.

That's just the kind of player Sakic was throughout his career. He could do it all on the ice, and he did it in a selfless manner.

#43

Peter Forsberg

Eleven seasons with Quebec Nordiques/Colorado Avalanche. Two seasons with Philadelphia Flyers. One season with Nashville Predators.

P eter Forsberg started his career as one of the handful of assets that was traded to the Quebec Nordiques when Eric Lindros refused to sign with the team that drafted him.

Forsberg was the sixth player taken in the 1991 draft, and it seems quite obvious that the Philadelphia Flyers didn't realize the talent they had within their grasp. Forsberg had size, strength, speed, and skill in abundance, and he projected to be a productive NHL player.

Peter Forsberg

However, the Flyers and most other teams looked at Lindros as a once-in-a-generation type of player—perhaps a Wayne Gretzky or Mario Lemieux with muscles—and they put together a huge trade package to entice the Nordiques to give them the rights to Lindros.

Quebec made the deal, and it turned out to be the trade that made the franchise one of the elite teams in the NHL.

Unfortunately for the

Career regular season:
708 games, 249 goals, 636 assists, 885 points
One-time Calder Trophy winner (Rookie of the Year)
One-time Hart Trophy winner (MVP)
One-time Ross Trophy winner (Leading Scorer)
Three-time first-team NHL All-Star
Two-time Stanley Cup winner
Elected to Hall of Fame in 2014
Advanced stats: 77.4 OPS, 20.6 DPS, 98.0 PS

people of Quebec, the Nordiques had their glory years as the Colorado Avalanche, and unfortunately for the Philadelphia Flyers, the talented Lindros wouldn't reach the heights that many had expected.

Forsberg didn't meet expectations, either. He exceeded them by a wide margin.

Injuries prevented him from having a long career, but he was brilliant when he was on the ice for the Nordiques and the Avalanche. He stayed in his native Sweden until January of 1995, and that's when he reported to Quebec. The first half of the 1994–95 season was eliminated by the NHL's decision to lock out its players, but once the work stoppage ended, Forsberg had the opportunity to show what he could do against North American players.

Forsberg scored 15 goals and 35 assists as a rookie, and that was good enough to earn him the Calder Trophy. The Nordiques made the playoffs that season for the first time in many years, and while they were eliminated in six games by the New York Rangers, Forsberg scored two goals and four assists and served notice that he would be a dominating postseason performer in the years to come.

The Nords moved to Colorado the following year, and the team was ready to come of age in the 1995–96 season. Forsberg turned into a full-fledged superstar, and he had a brilliant partner in Joe Sakic. With those two players leading the way, the Avalanche won the Pacific Division with 104 points.

While they had a brilliant year, nobody expected them to win the Stanley Cup because the Detroit Red Wings had won the President's Trophy with a huge 131-point season. Nobody was expected to even push the Wings to the limit, but the Avs were not impressed.

After they defeated the Vancouver Canucks and Chicago Blackhawks—both in six games—the Avs faced off against the Red Wings for the Western Conference title. Shockingly, the Avs won the first two games of the series at the Joe Louis Arena in Detroit, and they went on to win the series in six games.

After that huge victory, the Avs had no problems winning their first Stanley Cup, as they blitzed the Florida Panthers 4-0 in the Stanley Cup Final.

Forsberg had scored 30 goals and 86 assists in the regular season, and while it didn't come close to Lemieux's 161 points, it firmly established him as one of the most explosive and creative players in the league. He was also brilliant in the postseason, scoring 10 goals and 11 assists. Forsberg scored on an eye-catching 20 percent of the shots on goal he had taken.

Forsberg's brilliance came as much from his intelligence on the ice as his skating and playmaking ability. He had the ability to figure out where the play was going, and he would put his passes in a place where he knew his teammates were going to be.

That passing foresight and accuracy allowed the Avs to make plays that few other teams could even conceive of. Forsberg would score 90-plus points in 1997–98 and 1998–99, but the Avs could not follow up on their initial Stanley Cup success. They lost to the Edmonton Oilers in '98, and they were eliminated by the Dallas Stars in the seventh game of the Western Conference Final the following year.

If that loss didn't hurt enough, the Avs suffered another seven-game loss to Dallas in 2000 in the Conference Final again. Forsberg was limited by injuries to 49 games that year, but he once again asserted himself in the postseason with seven goals and eight assists.

There would be no denying the Avs in 2000–01, as they were motivated by the acquisition of Ray Bourque, and they wanted to get the former Boston Bruin his first Stanley Cup. Forsberg had an excellent season with 27 goals and 62 assists, and he started the playoffs with a rush. He scored four goals and 10 assists, and he scored the first playoff overtime goal of his career.

However, as the Avs were outlasting the Los Angeles Kings in seven games, Forsberg suffered a severe spleen injury and had to have it removed. He was out for the playoffs and had to watch his teammates beat the St. Louis Blues in the Western Conference Final and the New Jersey Devils in the championship round.

That injury also forced him to miss the 2001–02 regular season, but he was in top form when he returned for the playoffs. Playing with courage and hunger, Forsberg scored nine goals and 18 assists in the postseason, and his 27 points led all playoff performers. However, the Avs were eliminated in the Western Conference final by the Red Wings in seven games. Detroit took the decisive game by a 7-0 margin.

Forsberg was healthy and ready to play at the start of the 2002–03 season, and he had a banner year with 29 goals and 77 assists. Not only did he win the Ross Trophy as the league's leading scorer, but he also came home with the Hart Trophy.

That was Forsberg's last brilliant season with the Avs. He was limited to 39 games the next year due to injuries, and the 2004–05 season was lost due to yet another lockout.

When that finally ended, the Avs were burdened by salary-cap issues and they were forced to trade Forsberg to Philadelphia, the team that had drafted him so many years ago.

Forsberg played well for the Flyers over a brief stay, but he was no longer the game-changing player he had been with the Avs. He moved on to Nashville before returning to Colorado and retiring in 2010–11.

Forsberg had made his mark on the NHL, and if he had been able to avoid injuries and two lockouts, his footprint would have been even larger.

#44

Dominik Hasek

Nine seasons with Buffalo Sabres. Four seasons with Detroit Red Wings. Two seasons with Chicago Blackhawks. One season with Ottawa Senators.

I t's quite clear that when Dominik Hasek was drafted into the NHL, he did it with little fanfare.

He was viewed as a talented goaltending prospect from Czecho-slovakia who would have a chance to become a very good NHL goaltender, but there were no guarantees that he would ever leave his native country and that's why he was not selected until the tenth round of the 1983 draft by the Chicago Blackhawks.

Dominik Hasek

However, while it was quite challenging to get players from countries behind the Iron Curtain to go to North America at that time, neither Hasek nor the Blackhawks ever gave up. While he stayed in Czechoslovakia to play for his home country in international competitions like the Olympics and World Championships as well as in European-based regular-season hockey, he eventually made it across the Atlantic.

Hasek immediately flashed his talent with the Blackhawks, but he displayed little of the consistency that would eventually turn him into one of the greatest goalies in the history of the sport. The Blackhawks gave him a chance to play five games in the 1990-91 season and 20 more the following season, but he spent most of those two years shuttling between Chicago and Indianapolis where he was playing with the Blackhawks' minor-league team.

Career regular season:
735 games, 389-223-95, 2.20 goals-against average, .922 save percentage, 81 shutouts
Six-time Vezina Trophy winner (Top Goaltender)
Two-time Hart Trophy winner (MVP)
Two-time Ted Lindsay Award winner (Most Outstanding Player)
Three-time William Jennings Trophy winner (Fewest Goals Allowed)
Seven-time first-team NHL All-Star
Two-time Stanley Cup winner
Elected to Hall of Fame in 2014

After waiting so many years for Hasek to join the organization, the Blackhawks decided to pull the plug on Hasek and they traded him to the Buffalo Sabres in 1992 for goalie Stephane Beauregard and a fourth-round draft choice that Chicago ultimately used to draft big winger Eric Daze.

Remember, this is the team that traded away Phil Esposito to the Boston Bruins. This trade was nearly as damaging as that one.

Hasek would go on to make a name for himself and become one of the elite goalies in the league while playing for the Sabres. When he joined the Sabres, the team also had former Edmonton Oilers star Grant Fuhr in goal, and while Fuhr was still technically the No. 1 goalie, Hasek got the chance to play regularly and prove himself.

He became the team's No. 1 goalie by the 1993–94 season, and he was simply dominant. Hasek had a 30-20-6 record for the Sabres that season, and his statistics were beyond impressive. He had a 1.95 goals-against average, a scintillating .930 save percentage, and he recorded seven shutouts.

Hasek opened eyes all over the league with his performance, and he earned first-team All-Star status, the Vezina Trophy as the NHL's best goaltender, and the Jennings Trophy because the Sabres gave up fewer goals than any other team in the league.

While the numbers were sensational, his style of play was unlike any other goalie in the league. Instead of maintaining perfect lines and cutting off the shooter's angle, Hasek almost challenged shooters by giving them a spot to shoot at, then taking it away at a critical moment.

He did that with remarkable athleticism and quickness, and sensational reflexes that led to acrobatic saves. Unlike most goalies, Hasek often found himself on the highlight films because he would literally dive and throw himself at the puck in order to keep it out of the net.

Critics quickly emerged and said that Hasek's quirky style would not work in the NHL and that while he might have a good season here or there, he would not be able to sustain his success. NHL shooters were simply too good not to figure him out.

That theory quickly went out the window as Hasek gave the Sabres sensational goaltending every year. They knew that if they could just play a half-decent game, Hasek would give them a chance to win every night.

Hasek was not just a great NHL goaltender, he was completely dominant, and "The Dominator" won the Vezina Trophy five times over a six-year period. No other goaltender—including Ken Dryden, Patrick Roy, Bernie Parent, and Martin Brodeur—has ever come close to such a streak.

Dominik Hasek

In addition to establishing himself as the league's best goaltender, Hasek won the Hart Trophy in 1996–97 and '97–98. Hasek had a 2.27 GAA with a .930 save percentage and five shutouts in his first MVP season, and he silenced all critics the following year when he had 2.09 GAA with a .932 save percentage and a shocking 13 shutouts. That was the most shutouts by any NHL goaltender since Tony Esposito had registered 15 with the Blackhawks in 1969–70.

The longer Hasek played, the more he wanted to taste the glory that came with winning a Stanley Cup.

The Sabres were a playoff team throughout Hasek's run with them, but they were not a championship team. The Sabres got close in the 1997–98 season when they routed the Philadelphia Flyers and Montreal Canadiens in the first two rounds of the playoffs, but they were stopped by the Washington Capitals in the Eastern Conference Final and denied an opportunity to go to the Stanley Cup Final.

The following year, the determination coming from Hasek was palpable. After getting to the Conference final, he wanted more. Once again, the Sabres took care of business by disposing of the Ottawa Senators in the opening round and then surviving a tough six-game matchup with the Boston Bruins in the second round.

They also handled their business by beating the Toronto Maple Leafs in five games in the Eastern Conference Final, and earned a spot to play the Dallas Stars for the Stanley Cup.

Hasek was once again at his best with the championship on the line. However, the Stars were led by Mike Modano, Brett Hull, and an excellent goaltender in Ed Belfour, and outlasted the Sabres in six games as Hull scored a controversial series-winner in triple overtime.

Hasek was heartbroken by the loss and hungered for the chance to play for a championship team. He was eventually traded to the Detroit Red Wings, who had become the best team in the league and were a perennial title contender.

Hasek finally got his Stanley Cup following the 2001–02 season. He had been solid during the regular season, but he was thirty-seven years old and he didn't seem to have the reflexes that he had displayed in his glory years with the Sabres.

But if there were any doubts about his ability, he silenced them with his performance in the playoffs. He had a 1.86 GAA and a .920 save percentage and registered six shutouts in the postseason as the Red Wings won the Stanley Cup by surviving a classic Western Conference Final against the Colorado Avalanche in seven games and then taking care of business against the overmatched Carolina Hurricanes in five games.

Hasek would also be part of another Stanley Cup run for the Red Wings in 2007–08, but by then he had ceded the net to Chris Osgood.

Hasek retired after that season, but his reputation as the most acrobatic goalie in league history was secure and he earned Hall of Fame status in 2014.

#45

Grant Fuhr

Ten seasons with Edmonton Oilers. Four seasons with St. Louis Blues. Three seasons with Buffalo Sabres. Two seasons with Toronto Maple Leafs. One season with Calgary Flames. One season with Los Angeles Kings.

There is no better label a netminder can have than being called a money goalie.

It means that when the game is on the line, he is going to come up with the big save. It means when it's the late stages of a one-goal game in the playoffs, he is not going to let anything slip by. It means

Career regular season:
868 games, 403-295-114, 3.38 goals-against average, 25 shutouts
One-time Vezina Trophy winner (Top Goaltender)
One-time Jennings Trophy winner (Fewest Goals Against)
One-time first-team NHL All-Star, One-time second-team NHL All-Star
Four-time Stanley Cup winner
Elected to Hall of Fame in 2003

that when the Stanley Cup is on the line, he is going to button up all the openings and make every save he has to in order to get his team a victory.

Grant Fuhr was a money goalie. Playing for the high-scoring and dramatically explosive Edmonton Oilers didn't mean he had to have a scintillating goals-against average. There were many times that Fuhr had very ordinary numbers.

However, when he had to come up with the big save by kicking out his pad or flashing his glove, Fuhr was regularly the best goalie in the world. He was the perfect goalie for the Oilers.

He was loose and fun-loving, and he was one of the guys. Goaltenders are often separate from the team and are dramatic about their preparations, but that was not the way Fuhr went about his business. He knew he was surrounded by great teammates like Wayne Gretzky, Mark Messier, Glenn Anderson, Paul Coffey, and Jari Kurri, and his main job was to stop the puck, but he enjoyed playing with those players and winning championships.

Fuhr was the first black superstar in the NHL, but he always claimed publicly that race was not important to him. He downplayed his role as a trailblazer for other black players, and when he did talk about it, he deflected the credit to former Boston Bruin Willie O'Ree, who was the first black player in the league.

However, it was Fuhr who eventually made the Hall of Fame, and he was the first African-Canadian player in the Toronto shrine.

Fuhr had flashed his talent as a junior player, and Oilers general manager/head coach Glen Sather liked what he saw when he watched Fuhr in the net. Sather selected Fuhr with the eighth pick

Grant Fuhr

in the 1981 draft, and most observers thought Sather had come up with a brilliant selection and that Fuhr would be a can't-miss pick.

In his early years, Fuhr and Andy Moog shared much of the goaltending duties for the Oilers, but when the team got to the postseason, Fuhr regularly got the nod.

Even though the Oilers were the highest-scoring team in the league, they were not an easy team for a goaltender to play for. Certainly, Fuhr would often have a big lead in a game, but the Oilers were so offensive-minded that they left their goaltender with several odd-man rushes to contend with in nearly every game. Goaltenders who face breakaways, two-on-ones, and three-on-twos are going to give up their fair share of goals over the course of a season. But Fuhr knew that was all part of the deal of playing goal for the Oilers.

There was not going to be a lot of strong defensive play and the tendency to give up scoring opportunities was just something he had to live with.

That's why Fuhr never had a scintillating goals-against average during the regular season. He played in a high-scoring era for an offense-first team, and he regularly gave up 3.50 goals per game. His best mark with the Oilers was 3.43 in the 1987–88 season, but he played 75 games that season and he put together a 40-24-9 record with four shutouts.

Fuhr regularly acknowledged that the Oilers didn't necessarily need great goaltending in the regular season. However, the playoffs are another story. Edmonton did not necessarily tighten up the defense and play typical playoff hockey just because they were involved in a best-of-seven series. However, there were moments throughout the game when Fuhr had to make big saves to either preserve or reverse momentum.

The Oilers won four Stanley Cups during Fuhr's run in Edmonton, and he was the primary goaltender in all of them. He was a twenty-one-year-old goalie when the Oilers won their first championship in 1984, and he had an 11-4 record with a 2.99 GAA as the Oilers finally got to the top of the mountain by dethroning the four-time Stanley Cup champion New York Islanders.

The next season, Fuhr was 15–3 in the postseason with a 3.10 GAA. The Oilers pummeled the Philadelphia Flyers in five games in the championship round, and while there was no denying Gretzky, Messier, and Co., it was Fuhr who came up with the key saves that prevented the Flyers from getting back in the series at any time.

Fuhr backstopped the Oilers to two more Cups in 1987 and '88, and the last of those championships saw Fuhr in net for all 16 postseason victories. The Boston Bruins provided the opposition in that championship run, and they had a hard time getting control of the puck against Gretzky's last team. However, whenever the Bruins mounted an assault on the net, Fuhr stopped them.

In addition to his Stanley Cups, Fuhr got the nod in the Canada Cup prior to the 1987–88 season. It was a spectacular team that featured Gretzky and Mario Lemieux playing on the same line, but Canada was playing against a very talented Russian team.

The Russians came at Fuhr with rush after rush, but he made acrobatic saves and he did not let in any soft goals. Fuhr had a 6-1-2 record in the series, and his consistent play was one of the main reasons Canada was victorious in the memorable tournament.

Fuhr had personnel difficulties with cocaine toward the end of his career in Edmonton and he was traded by the Oilers to Toronto before the 1991–92 season. He was traded along with Anderson and Craig Berube and it was more about a sell-off of talent rather than punishment for his problem.

Fuhr later played for the Buffalo Sabres, Los Angeles Kings, St. Louis Blues, and Calgary Flames. While he would occasionally show off his talent, his best tenure came during those championship years with the Oilers.

He proved himself to be a great money goalie, and that's just what Gretzky and Co. needed.

#46

Sergei Fedorov

Thirteen seasons with Detroit Red Wings. Three seasons with Columbus Blue Jackets. Two seasons with Mighty Ducks of Anaheim. Two seasons with Washington Capitals.

It's so much easier for modern-day players to move from Russia to play in the NHL if they so choose than it was in the past. As long as the talent level is there and an NHL team drafts a Russian player, he can choose to play in North America.

But it was not always like that, and in the late 1980s, it was not always legal for players to leave Russia and play in the United States

Career regular season:
1,248 games, 483 goals, 696 assists, 1,179 points
Two-time Frank Selke Trophy winner (Best Defensive Forward)
One-time Ted Lindsay Award winner (Most Outstanding Player)
One-time Hart Trophy winner (MVP)
One-time first-team NHL All-Star
Three-time Stanley Cup champion
Advanced stats: 96.0 OPS, 29.6 DPS, 125.6 PS
Elected to Hall of Fame in 2015

and Canada. That's why the Detroit Red Wings drafted Sergei Fedorov in the fourth round. He was perhaps the most talented player in the 1989 draft, but the Red Wings had no assurances that Fedorov would be able to leave Russia and put a Red Wings uniform on over his head.

It didn't matter that Fedorov wanted to play in North America, because Viktor Tikhonov did not want to allow his players to leave the Soviet national team and play for big money in the NHL.

He would entice them to stay with promises of benefits like bigger apartments and cars, and he would threaten them by saying they would never play with the national team in the Olympics and other big tournaments.

However, Fedorov and other stars knew what they wanted. They wanted the freedom of playing in North America and they wanted to test themselves by playing against the best competition in the world.

After Fedorov's friend and former roommate Alexander Mogilny defected during a tour of North America, it seemed like it was just a matter of time before Fedorov would do the same.

It happened in 1990, after Fedorov's military service requirements had been fulfilled. He was with the Soviet team at the Goodwill Games in Seattle, and once he travelled with that unit to Portland, Oregon, he used that opportunity to sign a contract with the Red Wings.

Once he signed his deal with Detroit, Fedorov took a deep breath, started moving at full speed, and attacked his new career in North America.

Sergei Fedorov

"I wasn't scared when I left the Russian team, but I was really excited," Fedorov said. "Sometimes the less you know, the better. All I could think about was playing in big NHL arenas and that's why I wasn't scared. Perhaps I didn't know any better."

Fedorov was a brilliant player right from the start. He had all the tools needed to succeed. He was a brilliant skater, both in terms of speed and agility. He could slow it down so he could make a gravity-defying cut on the ice and then explode out of the move and sprint toward the opposing net.

He had a remarkable number of shots at his disposal. He had a quick wrist shot and a whistling snap shot that regularly handcuffed goalies. His backhand was magical as he could go to the top corner from 20 feet or more, and he may have had the most accurate slap-shot in the last thirty years.

The slapshot is not usually as consistent as a wrist or snap shot because it's more difficult to control where it's going. But Fedorov was able to extend his left (bottom) hand on his stick and that would give him more precision than the average player. If Fedorov recognized that a goalie was giving him six inches of extra space on the far side, he could regularly hit that opening.

Fedorov scored 31 goals and 48 assists in his rookie season, and his 79-point season earned him a second-place finish in the Calder Trophy voting behind Chicago goalie Ed Belfour.

Fedorov also came along at a time when the Red Wings were improving every season and adding impressive talent. Many of the Red Wings' new stars were Soviet imports, and that gave the team greater depth and presence every year.

Fedorov was thrilled to play with former Soviet stars like Igor Larionov, Viacheslav Fetisov, Vladimir Konstantinov, and Vyacheslov Kozlov, and there were times that Red Wings head coach Scotty Bowman would use those five players as the team's most effective power play unit. The "Russian Five" played a big role for the Red Wings as the team became dominant in the 1990s.

Fedorov would become one of the top stars in the game. After breaking through the 30-goal mark in his second and third years with the Wings, he raised his game to a new level in 1993–94 when he scored 56 goals and 64 assists. Fedorov was voted as the Hart Trophy winner that year, and was the first ex-Soviet player to win that honor. He also won the Frank Selke Trophy and the Ted Lindsay Award as the NHL's most outstanding player.

The Selke Trophy was significant because it went to the best defensive forward, and for Fedorov to win both the Hart and Selke Trophies in the same year was unprecedented. His versatility played a key role in the Red Wings 100-point season. However, even though they had the best record in the Western Conference, they were bounced from the playoffs by the upstart San Jose Sharks in the first round.

That loss helped steel the team and get them ready to win championships. That happened in 1996–97, and Fedorov played a huge role. He scored 30 goals and 33 assists during the regular season and regularly handled the Red Wings' toughest defensive assignments. He also scored eight goals and 12 assists in the playoffs as Detroit swept Philadelphia in the Stanley Cup Final.

The Red Wings became repeat champions with another brilliant run through the playoffs that culminated with another Stanley Cup Final sweep. The Red Wings were just too quick, clever, and opportunistic for the Washington Capitals, and Fedorov was dynamic in the postseason after an injury-plagued regular season. Fedorov had 10 goals and 10 assists in that championship run.

The Red Wings also won another championship with Fedorov in 2001–02, as Fedorov scored 31 goals and 32 assists, and he contributed five goals and 14 assists in the playoffs.

Fedorov remained with the Red Wings through the 2002–03 season, when he scored 36 goals and 47 assists. The Mighty Ducks of Anaheim signed him as a free agent after that season, and he was later traded to the Columbus Blue Jackets and the Washington Capitals.

But his biggest and best impact came with the Red Wings, and the three-time Stanley Cup champion was one of the greatest two-way players the game has seen.

#47

Yvan Cournoyer

Sixteen seasons with Montreal Canadiens.

When it comes to sheer speed and artistry on the ice, few players have ever been able to get close to Yvan Cournoyer.

The Montreal Canadiens have long been known as the Flying Frenchmen, and Cournoyer is right at the top of the pack when it comes to instant acceleration and the ability to speed up and down the ice.

While Cournoyer is one of the great players in Montreal history, his tenure in Montreal didn't start out so terrific. He was a rookie in the 1964–65 season, but there was definitely a chill coming from

Career regular season:
968 games, 428 goals, 436 assists,
863 points
One-time Conn Smythe Trophy
winner (Playoff MVP)
Four-time second-team NHL
All-Star
10-time Stanley Cup champion
**Advanced stats: 72.6 OPS,
18.7 DPS, 91.3 PS**
Elected to Hall of Fame in 1982

legendary Habs coach Toe Blake and being sent toward Cournoyer.

Blake could see his rookie's blazing speed and offensive skill, but he thought Cournoyer was too care-free and that he was not a responsible player on the defensive end. As a result, he was used almost exclusively on the power play in those early years.

The fans at the Montreal Forum were not satisfied that Cournoyer was getting limited playing time. They wanted to see him take a regular shift and consistently demanded that Blake put him on the ice when they chanted, "We Want Cournoyer."

Blake would bristle, claiming that he was trying to protect the speedster and keep him from getting exposed. At one point, the Habs sent Cournoyer down to the American Hockey League so he could work on the defensive aspects of the game, and that taught him that he would have to do whatever he could to stay with the big club for the rest of his career.

"I knew then that the only place to be was with the big team," Cournoyer said. "I guess I always knew that, but it had never occurred to me that I might not be a part of it. When I got back, I said to myself, 'Yvan, this is the only place to be and you are going to work hard to be here.' Maybe it was then that I started to mature. Toe kept harping at my defensive play, and I kept working on it."

Eventually, Cournoyer's playing time would increase, but he wouldn't take a full-time, regular shift until Blake retired following the Habs' 1968 Stanley Cup. New coach Claude Ruel did not exactly distinguish himself with a long run in Montreal, but he had enough sense to make Cournoyer a featured performer.

Yvan Cournoyer

That's when Cournoyer tuned himself into a legitimate NHL superstar. He scored 43 goals and 44 assists that season, and eight of his goals were game-winners for the Canadiens. He was still a power play fixture and he scored 14 of his goals with the man advantage, but his 29 goals at even strength showed that Cournoyer was dangerous every time he stepped onto the ice.

In addition to his offensive skills, "The Roadrunner" used his explosive speed to become a much better defensive player. Cournoyer became an excellent back checker who could see what his opponents were doing when they moved into the offensive zone, and he diagnosed their plans and got his stick in the passing lanes. He had the ability to intercept passes and allow the Canadiens to quickly turn defense into offense.

In addition to his speed, Cournoyer had remarkable skills at stick-handling. He had the ability to make opposing defensemen look ridiculous because he could turn them inside out. If a great basketball player like Chris Paul of the Los Angeles Clippers can "break ankles" with his ability to fake out a defender, Cournoyer was hockey's equivalent of that.

There may be several great stickhandlers in today's game like Chicago's Patrick Kane or Tampa Bay's Tyler Johnson. However, none of those players could compare with Cournoyer. Both of those players excel at making two or three quick moves; Cournoyer could string together five or six fakes before he made a pass or let go of his shot.

When Cournoyer was in full flight, he was appreciated by all fans. In 1977, he was playing a game at Madison Square Garden and he made a big circle around the New York net as he attempted to find an open teammate or take a shot. However, the New York defense held tight and didn't give Cournoyer an option he liked. So he made another huge circle around the New York net before he finally got rid of the puck.

When he finally did, the Rangers fans stood on their feet and gave him an ovation normally reserved for one of their own heroes.

Cournoyer scored 40 or more goals from 1971–72 through 1973–74. He scored a career-best 47 goals in 1971–72. His distinctive style made him one of the most widely recognized players every time he stepped on the ice, but he was far more than an individual star.

He was a huge presence in the locker room and was eventually named captain of the team in 1975 after Henri Richard retired.

Cournoyer's presence had a remarkable impact on the Canadiens. He played fifteen seasons in Montreal and the Habs won the Stanley Cup in ten of those years.

"After you win one, you want to win again. It proves you're the best in the world," Cournoyer states. "If you see teams like the Islanders, Pittsburgh, Oilers—after they won the Stanley Cup, they won it again because after you've tasted it, it's hard not to try to win the Stanley Cup again. To be recognized, you have to win the Stanley Cup. That's why you play the game."

Even as Cournoyer reached the final years of his career, he still had bursts of the eye-catching quickness that made him one of the most exciting and productive players in the league. But years of playing at top speed had taken a toll on his body, and Cournoyer was forced to play with consistent and brutal back pain in his final seasons.

The Habs had just won their third straight Stanley Cup in 1978, but he was laboring through that run and the pain in his back became too much to bear. After undergoing two different bouts of back surgery, he was forced to retire after playing just 15 games in 1978–79.

He left the Canadiens as one of the true legends for one of the most accomplished franchises in the history of the NHL.

#48

Dave Keon

Fifteen seasons with Toronto Maple Leafs. Three seasons with Hartford Whalers. Four seasons in World Hockey Association (New England Whalers, Indianapolis Racers, Minnesota Fighting Saints).

There was a time when the Toronto Maple Leafs really were the national team of Canada.

There was a time when the Blue and White stood for something meaningful in the world of hockey and did not just go through the motions in the second half of the year as they did in 2014–15.

Career regular season:

NHL Career: 1,296 games, 396 goals, 590 assists, 986 points

WHA: 301 games, 182 goals, 189 assists, 291 points

One-time Calder Trophy winner (Rookie of the Year)

One-time Conn Smythe Trophy winner (Playoff MVP)

Two-time Lady Byng Trophy winner (Gentlemanly Play)

Two-time Paul Deneau Trophy winner (WHA Gentlemanly Play)

Two-time second-team NHL All-Star

Four-time Stanley Cup champion

Advanced stats: 66.9 OPS, 19.6 DPS, 86.5 PS

Elected to Hall of Fame in 1986

There was a time when the Toronto Maple Leafs played their best hockey in the playoffs, ground down opponents, and forced them to give up big leads in the third period, unlike the 2012–13 Maple Leafs, who blew a three-goal lead in the third period of the seventh game against the Boston Bruins in one of the NHL's most notable choke jobs.

It's been a long time, but the Maple Leafs ruled the NHL through much of the 1960s, and while they had many good and exciting players, the best and most important was center Dave Keon.

Smart, swift, resourceful, and dependable, Keon was the fastest of the Leafs and he had a nose for where the puck was going to be. He didn't waste time chasing after the puck; he skated to where it was going to be next. His instincts were developed to the fullest, and even though he was 5-9 and 180 pounds, he was strong enough to carry the Leafs on his shoulders for many nights.

Keon grew up in Quebec, and many of the best hockey-playing youngsters were quickly under the aura of the Montreal Canadiens. But at an early part of his development, the Detroit Red Wings were hot to sign Keon and they wanted him badly.

However, Detroit was an awfully long way from his home in Noranda, Quebec, and Keon's mother did not want him moving that far away. Instead of signing with the Red Wings, Keon opted

Dave Keon

to play for St. Michael's College, and that institution had served as a pipeline for the Maple Leafs. Playing in Toronto was much more favorable as far as Keon's mother was concerned.

Keon had been an offensive juggernaut prior to getting to St. Michael's, but he had not paid much attention to defense at that point. However, when he was informed that playing hard-nosed defense was the difference between playing in the NHL the next year or the minor leagues, he quickly learned how to play in his own zone and break up opponents' offensive thrusts on a consistent basis.

He was signed by the Leafs and played a key role for them as a twenty-year-old rookie in the 1960–61 season. He scored 20 goals and 25 assists and played all 70 games. He became a mainstay for the Leafs early that year and won the Calder Trophy.

The Leafs finished second in the regular season that year, just two points behind the Montreal Canadiens. It was expected that the Leafs would beat the fourth-place Red Wings in the first round and the Habs would beat the Chicago Blackhawks, but the underdogs won both series. Toronto lost in five games, and the team was quite disappointed with their showing.

Keon was fully established by the start of his second season, and he pushed the Leafs hard. He scored 26 goals and 35 assists and earned second-team All-Star status as well as the Lady Byng Trophy. The Leafs once again finished second to Montreal in the regular season.

The determined Keon was on top of his game when the Leafs got to the playoffs, as he scored five goals and three assists. They were not about to lose their first-round matchup with the New York Rangers, and they eliminated the Broadway Blueshirts in six games.

The defending champion Chicago Blackhawks appeared to be a formidable opponent in the Stanley Cup Final with superstars Bobby Hull and Stan Mikita, but Toronto took the title in six games.

Keon continued to play a key role with the Leafs, along with high-scoring left wing Frank Mahovlich. Keon scored 28 goals and 28 assists as the Leafs took first place in the 1962–63 season and won their second consecutive Stanley Cup as they whipped the Red Wings in five games in the championship round.

Keon had developed a brilliant backhand shot that was both powerful and accurate. Keon sensed that most goalies weren't expecting that shot, and that's why he spent so much time practicing it.

"Most kids today slap the puck," Keon said. "The backhand takes time to learn. It's not something you do naturally. But it is an effective shot."

It wasn't unusual for a team to win two championships in a row through the early 1960s, but to be recognized as a dynasty that could compare with the great Montreal teams led by Jean Beliveau and Maurice Richard or the powerful Red Wings teams led by Gordie Howe, the Leafs would have to make it three in a row.

The consistent Keon was once again a mainstay in 1963–64, as he scored 23 goals and 37 assists. The Leafs were just a third-place team that season, and they were sizable underdogs in their first-round matchup with the Canadiens. However, the Maple Leafs extended the series to a seventh game and whipped Montreal on its home ice in seven games.

That propelled the Maple Leafs to the Stanley Cup Final yet again, and they edged the Red Wings in seven games. Keon was once again magnificent with seven goals and two assists while playing marvelous defense.

The Leafs' championship run was derailed in 1965, but they won their fourth title in the decade in the 1966–67 season, the last year before the NHL expanded from six to twelve teams.

Keon was a dynamic force on the team and his defense was scintillating by that point. He scored 19 goals and 33 assists, and he had the responsibility of checking the opponents' top center.

He excelled at the job, and he was at his best in the playoffs when he was on top of his game with three goals and five assists. Toronto took care of Chicago in six games in the first round and also eliminated the Canadiens in six games. Keon won the Conn Smythe Trophy for his brilliant all-around play.

The Leafs have not won another Stanley Cup since, but they got several more excellent years out of Keon, including his brilliant

Dave Keon

1970–71 season in which he scored 38 goals and 38 assists. He was nearly as good two years later when he tallied 37 goals and 36 assists.

He was the Leafs' best and most dependable player, but by the summer of 1975, hard-boiled owner Harold Ballard was bound and determined to rebuild the team and he let Keon go unsigned. Keon played the next four seasons in the World Hockey Association before returning to the NHL for his final years with the Hartford Whalers.

But Keon is best remembered as the captain of the Leafs and a four-time Stanley Cup champion. He was elected to the Hall of Fame in 1986, and it seems like the Leafs have not had a player with his unique talents in decades.

The phrase is used constantly in today's game to describe players like Jonathan Toews, Patrice Bergeron, and Anze Kopitar, but Dave Keon was one of the greatest two-way players of his era.

#49

Jean Ratelle

Sixteen seasons with New York Rangers. Five seasons with Boston Bruins.

Jean Ratelle was to the New York Rangers and later to the Boston Bruins what Jean Beliveau was to the Montreal Canadiens.

Both men played brilliantly in the NHL and dominated on the scoresheet and with their all-around play. Both were considered gentlemen who were always calm and cool under pressure.

The only difference between the two: Beliveau played on ten Canadiens teams that won the Stanley Cup. While Ratelle got close with both the Rangers and the Bruins, he didn't win any.

Jean Ratelle

It was clearly a regret for the graceful center, but his peers and coaches admired his career. Ratelle's career began when he was brought up to the NHL by the New York Rangers in 1960–61, but he didn't establish himself as a vital player for the Blueshirts until the 1965–66 season when he scored 21 goals and 30 assists.

The Rangers were a non-playoff team through the early part of Ratelle's career, but general man-

Career regular season:
1,281 games, 491 goals, 776 assists, 1,267 points
One-time Bill Masterton Trophy winner
One-time Ted Lindsay Trophy winner (Rookie of the Year)
Two-time Lady Byng Memorial Trophy winner (Gentlemanly Play)
One-time second-team NHL All-Star
Advanced stats: 94.8 OPS, 24.3 DPS, 119.1 PS
Elected to Hall of Fame in 1985

ager Emile Francis was slowly but surely putting together a solid roster that was capable of playing with the better teams in the league.

The Rangers made the playoffs in 1966–67, and that marked the first of nine consecutive years that Ratelle would go to the post-season with the Rangers. While they were unsuccessful at first as they went up against opponents like the Canadiens, Chicago Black-hawks, and Bruins, the Rangers found their stride by the 1970–71 season, and they became one of the most formidable teams in the league.

Much of that was due to Ratelle, who was put on a line with childhood friend Rod Gilbert at right wing and Vic Hadfield at left wing. The trio knew each other's moves well, and they passed the puck smoothly. While Gilbert and Hadfield were both excellent players who could put the puck in the net with their big shots, it was Ratelle who was the best of the group.

He was simply a brilliant skater who could speed through the neutral zone and also slow down in order to get the defense off balance. He was a scintillating passer who put the puck where his linemates were going and his ability to hit them in stride made him one of the best players in the league.

Ratelle did not stop there. He rarely took slapshots, but he had one of the hardest and most accurate wrist shots in the league. He could fire the puck from a number of angles and he had a stellar backhand shot that was the envy of many players around the league.

The combination of Ratelle, Gilbert, and Hadfield took on the nickname of the GAG line, but it had nothing to do with the Rangers' propensity to come up short in the playoffs.

It stood for Goal A Game, because the Rangers could count on the trio to put at least one puck in the net every game.

That was not an accurate nickname for the unit in the 1971–72 season—because they scored a lot more than a goal a game. As the Rangers battled the Bruins for Eastern Conference supremacy, Ratelle and his linemates piled up points at an incredible rate. Hadfield and Gilbert were playing extremely well, but it was Ratelle who was opening eyes around the league with his explosiveness and his consistency.

As the season reached mid-February, Ratelle had already scored 46 goals and 63 assists. The 109 points represented a career high with nearly two months of the season to play, but he would not get another point in the regular season. Ratelle suffered a broken ankle and he would not be able to return until the playoffs.

Actually, Ratelle needed the Rangers to survive and advance in the postseason if he was going to play again. His teammates obliged, as the Rangers beat the Canadiens in the first round before sweeping the Blackhawks in the second round.

That allowed the Rangers to advance to the Stanley Cup Final for the first time since 1950. They met their archrivals from Boston, and the two teams were viewed as virtually even, especially with Ratelle returning.

While he was not at his best and his mobility was limited, the Bruins paid close attention to Ratelle everywhere he went. They held him to one goal in the six-game series.

In the end, the Rangers fell short against the Bruins, and most of that was due to the presence of Bobby Orr. The Rangers simply could not contain his speed, agility, and creativity, and he seemed to make the big play whenever the Bruins needed it.

The Rangers fell short in the playoffs in 1973, as they lost to Chicago after beating the Bruins in the first round. A year later, New York appeared poised to make its Stanley Cup run, but the Rangers lost to the Philadelphia Flyers in the semifinals in seven heart-wrenching games.

Things got even tougher in New York the following spring when the Rangers dropped their opening-round playoff series to the New York Islanders.

That defeat sent shockwaves through the Rangers and they ultimately dismantled the team. One of the biggest moves was a November 1975 trade that sent Ratelle, Brad Park, and Joe Zanussi to the Bruins for Phil Esposito and Carol Vadnais.

The trade was a shocker because of the enmity between the two teams, and few thought that Esposito would fit in with the Rangers or Park would adapt to the Bruins. There were never any questions about Ratelle, who continued to play stellar hockey after trading in his Ranger blues for the Black and Gold of the Bruins.

He quickly became one of the best players on the team, but once again luck worked against Ratelle. He thought his new team was capable of winning the Stanley Cups that eluded him in New York, but the Bruins' top weapon could no longer play. Orr's knees were shot, and Ratelle and Park were able to play just ten games with the brilliant defenseman.

Still, the Bruins were right at the top of the league for many years and Ratelle enjoyed five consecutive seasons with 25 goals or more. While the Rangers had often fallen short in terms of effort in the biggest moments, the Bruins rose to the occasion nearly every time.

However, while they were playing excellent hockey, they had to compete with the Canadiens when they were at their best. The Habs won four straight Stanley Cups, and two of them came against the Bruins in the Finals, while a third was perhaps the most painful loss of all.

That came in the 1979 semifinals, which was also the last year of Montreal's run. The Bruins and Canadiens had battled on even terms for six games, and the series came down to a seventh game in the Montreal Forum.

While normally this would be the end of the line for the Bruins, they took a 3-1 second period lead before Montreal tied it up. When Rick Middleton scored the go-ahead goal with 3:59 left, it appeared Boston had finally slayed the beast.

But an infamous too many men on the ice penalty against the Bruins gave Montreal a power play, and Guy Lafleur took advantage with a blistering shot that tied it up. While the Bruins had chances in the overtime period that followed, the Canadiens found a way to win when Yvon Lambert scored in the extra session.

Hearts sunk throughout Boston, and Ratelle's shoulders slumped as well. He played two more seasons in Boston before hanging up his skates, but that was his last legitimate chance to raise the Stanley Cup.

It never happened for Ratelle in his brilliant career, but he was truly one of the classiest players who ever laced up skates.

#50

Jonathan Toews
(through 2014–15)

Eight seasons with Chicago Blackhawks.

Jonathan Toews was a solid and promising hockey player when the Chicago Blackhawks selected him with the No. 3 pick in the 2006 draft.

They had high hopes that Toews would develop into a solid, two-way center with a bit of flair to his offensive game and more than a little bit of intensity to his defensive game.

Talk about getting a return on your investment!

Career regular season:
565 games, 223 goals, 283 assists, 510 points.
One-time Conn Smythe Trophy winner (Playoff MVP)
One-time Frank J. Selke Trophy winner (Best Defensive Forward)
One-time second-team NHL All-Star
Three-time Stanley Cup winner
Two-time Olympic Gold Medal winner
Advanced stats: 48.4 OPS, 17.9 DPS, 66.4 PS

Toews has turned into one of the National Hockey League's greatest stars and perhaps its best all-around player following the 2014–15 season. There are some who will still give Sidney Crosby the edge because he came into the league with more flair than Toews and as a greater offensive threat, but when it comes to coming up with dynamic plays that lead to winning, Toews doesn't have to take a back seat to Crosby.

Here's the bottom line: Toews may not be the best offensive player in hockey, as Crosby, Alex Ovechkin, Steven Stamkos, and Corey Perry may be more dangerous in the offensive zone. He may not be the best defensive forward in the game, as Patrice Bergeron may be slightly better. But when it comes to picking one player who can help a team win a game, a playoff series, or a Stanley Cup, there is no player who is more valuable in the NHL than Toews.

After getting drafted in 2006, Toews spent one more year playing at the University of North Dakota and for Canada's top junior team. However, the Blackhawks needed him badly and he was a rookie in 2007–08 along with running mate Patrick Kane.

At the time, there were whispers within the organization that Toews and Kane would do for the Chicago Blackhawks what Bobby Hull and Stan Mikita had done generations earlier.

But those were only whispers, because it seemed too good to be true. Mikita and Hull were legendary Hall of Famers who had been the most popular players on the team and in the league during the 1960s and early 1970s. While that team only won one Stanley Cup in 1961, they were perhaps the most exciting team in the league in those years and they came close to winning other championships.

To think that a pair of promising rookies could come close to matching them seemed ridiculous and was not worth saying out loud.

But those who were doing the whispering have been proven correct. Kane is a talented winger who may be the best stickhandler in the game since Wayne Gretzky was in his prime. He has speed and a slew of moves to go with an excellent shot. He has scored series-ending, dramatic goals throughout his career.

Toews does not necessarily have Kane's flair for the dramatic, but he cannot be topped when it comes to will, responsibility, and the ability to play his best when it matters most.

Toews scored 24 goals and 30 assists as a rookie, and he was so good and worked so hard in practice and in games that the Blackhawks named him the team's youngest captain in the organization's history when he was twenty.

His work ethic and maturity led to the nickname of Captain Serious, and he took his responsibilities, well, seriously.

Toews quickly became one of the most talked-about and feared players in the league because he was such a complete player. By the 2009–10 season, the Blackhawks were one of the best teams in the league, and much of that came from Toews' relentless drive on the ice.

Other coaches around the league noticed him, and when it came time to select players for Canada's Olympic hockey team, Toews was one of the first players chosen.

Toews was not cowed by the international stage. Playing in his home country, Toews proved to be one of the team's stars with a goal and seven assists as Canada won the gold medal and the nation rejoiced.

If 2010 got off to a good start for Toews, the finish of the NHL season was the stuff of dreams for Toews. The Blackhawks were second in the Western Conference at the end of the regular season behind the San Jose Sharks, and they were prepared for the playoffs.

They beat the Nashville Predators in six games and did the same with the Vancouver Canucks. Then came their confrontation with the Sharks, and it was expected to be a tight series that could go seven games.

The Blackhawks would have none of it, as they schooled the Sharks in four straight. They also took care of business against the upset-minded Philadelphia Flyers to win the Stanley Cup for the first time in forty-nine years.

Toews was simply sensational throughout the run. While Kane would have the honor of scoring the Stanley Cup-winning goals, Toews scored seven goals and added 22 assists in winning the Conn Smythe Trophy.

Three years later, the Blackhawks found themselves back in the Stanley Cup Final against an Original Six rival in the Boston Bruins. Boston had won the Stanley Cup in 2011, and both teams were hungry to add a second championship in a short span. The Bruins won two of the first three games and appeared to have command of the series as both teams prepared for Game 4 in Boston. Going into that game, Toews had been shackled by huge Boston defenseman Zdeno Chara, and the Blackhawks center came to the conclusion that the Blackhawks were giving him too much respect by trying to stay away from him.

Toews made up his mind to take the puck right at Chara and challenge him. The change in gameplan had a dramatic impact. Toews not only scored a key goal in Game 4, which Chicago eventually won in overtime, but also he showed that Chara was vulnerable, and that gave his teammates hope.

The Blackhawks swept the last three games of the series to take their second Stanley Cup in four years. Two years later, the Blackhawks found themselves in the Stanley Cup Final again.

This time they were confronted by an explosive and athletic team of young stars in the Tampa Bay Lightning. Interestingly, the series followed the same pattern as the Boston series did. The Blackhawks were down 2-1 after three games, but they won the final three games en route to their third Stanley Cup victory in six years.

Jonathan Toews (through 2014–15)

Toews had three goals and 11 assists in the 2013 playoffs and 10 goals and 11 assists in the 2015 triumph. At the conclusion of the sixth game in Chicago, NHL commissioner Gary Bettman called the Blackhawks a dynasty.

Toews was the first one to take the Stanley Cup from the commissioner in all three of the championship years.

While the media was not sure of whether the Blackhawks were a true dynasty, the labels didn't matter to Toews or his teammates. They merely wanted to win championships.

"This is why we play the game," Toews said. "You work hard all season just to get in this position and you sacrifice to get there. It's an incredible feeling and I wouldn't trade it for anything."

In his first eight seasons in the NHL, Toews has been a part of three Stanley Cup-winning teams and two Olympic gold medal-winning ones. At the age of twenty-seven, he may have ten to twelve good years remaining. He's already one of the top fifty players in the expansion era, and there's no telling how high he might be able to climb before he calls it a career.

INDEX

Index

Index